A History of the LMS:
The War Years and Nationalisation, 1939–48

'Steam Past' Books from Allen & Unwin

THE LIMITED by O. S. Nock
THE BIRTH OF BRITISH RAIL by Michael R. Bonavia
STEAM'S INDIAN SUMMER by George Heiron and Eric Treacy
GRAVEYARD OF STEAM by Brian Handley
PRESERVED STEAM IN BRITAIN by Patrick B. Whitehouse
MEN OF THE GREAT WESTERN by Peter Grafton
TRAVELLING BY TRAIN IN THE EDWARDIAN AGE by Philip Unwin
MAUNSELL'S NELSONS by D. W. Winkworth
MAN OF THE SOUTHERN: JIM EVANS LOOKS BACK by Jim Evans
TRAINS TO NOWHERE: BRITISH STEAM TRAIN ACCIDENTS 1906–1960 by J. A. B. Hamilton
TRAVELLING BY TRAIN IN THE 'TWENTIES AND 'THIRTIES by Philip Unwin
MEN OF THE LNER by Peter Grafton
A HISTORY OF THE LMS by O. S. Nock: I. The First Years, 1923–30
                                         II. The Record-Breaking 'Thirties, 1931–39
                                         III. The War Years and Nationalisation, 1939–48
A HISTORY OF THE LNER by Michael R. Bonavia: I. The Early Years, 1923–33
                                         II. The Years of Achievement, 1934–39
                                         III. The Last Years, 1939–48
ON AND OFF THE RAILS by Sir John Elliot
THE RIDDLES STANDARD TYPES IN TRAFFIC by G. Freeman Allen
THE SCHOOLS 4–4–0s by D. W. Winkworth
SOUTH WEST RAILWAYMAN by Donald King
LONDON MIDLAND MAIN LINE CAMERAMAN by W. Philip Conolly

A History of the LMS
III. The War Years and
Nationalisation, 1939-48

O. S. Nock B.Sc., C.Eng., F.I.C.E., F.I.Mech.E.

London
GEORGE ALLEN & UNWIN
Boston   Sydney

George Allen & Unwin (Publishers) Ltd,
40 Museum Street, London WC1A 1LU, UK

George Allen & Unwin (Publishers) Ltd,
Park Lane, Hemel Hempstead, Herts HP2 4TE, UK

Allen & Unwin Inc.,
9 Winchester Terrace, Winchester, Mass 01890, USA

George Allen & Unwin Australia Pty Ltd,
8 Napier Street, North Sydney, NSW 2060, Australia

First published in 1983

British Library Cataloguing in Publication Data

Nock, O. S.
  A History of the LMS.
Vol. 3
1. London, Midland and Scottish Railway – History
I. Title
358'.0941   HE3020.L75
ISBN 0–04–385097–9

Picture research by Mike Esau

Set in 10 on 12 point Bembo by Nene Phototypesetters Ltd
and printed in Great Britain
by Biddles Ltd, Guildford, Surrey

Contents

Illustrations

I
The First Four Months of War

Until the very last week before Great Britain declared war on Germany a sustained attempt was made to keep up a façade of normality in railway business, though at times the line of demarcation was growing perilously thin. I went to Dublin on 11 August, just before making some footplate runs on the new GSR 4–6–0 'Maeve', and travelling to Holyhead on the day Irish Mail I remember clearly conversations with fellow passengers about the black-out rehearsal that had taken place the previous evening. Just a week later Stanier left for the USA where he was to read a paper on 'Lightweight Passenger Rolling Stock' at the summer meeting of the Institution of Mechanical Engineers, to be held that year in New York. At the same time the Institution of Railway Signal Engineers held their summer meeting at Nottingham, and I was one of a party that visited the new mechanised marshalling yard at Toton, referred to in the concluding chapter of volume 2 of this work. Things were unhappily 'normal' in another respect in that a wage dispute led to ASLEF declaring a strike of its members from midnight on Saturday 26 August. Fortunately an appeal on humanitarian grounds – 'We may need you to get the children

away' – succeeded in getting the strike notices withdrawn, but it was a mighty close call. Within hours came news of the Russo-German 'entente', and an attack on Poland became inevitable.

On 1 September, the day of the first Nazi air raids on Warsaw and other Polish targets, the government took control of the British railways and the evacuation of children from London and other large centres of population began. In government circles it was thought quite possible that an attack on this country would be made without any formal declaration of war, and the armed forces and the civil defence services were already on full alert; but such an emergency did not, fortunately, occur and the evacuation of the children proceeded smoothly, without incident. The LMS share in this unprecedented feat of passenger transportation was to convey in the first four days of September approximately half-a-million people in 1,450 special trains. For three successive days London alone accounted for 160 outward trains, 115 on the Western and 45 on the Midland Divisions, and similar though less intensive movements were currently in progress from Birmingham, Bradford, Edinburgh, Glasgow, Leeds, Liverpool,

1. Air Raid Precautions – removing the glass from the station roof at Euston.

Manchester and Sheffield. From the railway operating point of view the job was not finished when the outward trains reached the reception areas. The coaching stock had to be worked back to the originating centres for more passengers on the following days.

The outbreak of war brought immediately a senior staff change of major importance. In 1937, largely at the instigation of Sir Nigel Gresley, but wholeheartedly supported on the LMS side by Sir Harold Hartley, the two companies had agreed jointly to the construction of a modern locomotive testing plant, to be located

at Rugby. R. C. Bond, until then Assistant Works Manager at Crewe, had been appointed Superintendent Engineer, reporting jointly to Stanier and Sir Nigel Gresley. By August 1939 work on the building had advanced considerably; but it was realised that the project would have to be suspended if war came, and sure enough no later than the morning of 4 September Bond was summoned to London to see Fairburn, who was Acting CME until Stanier returned from his abortive visit to New York. Before leaving Rugby Bond had been told by telephone that Riddles, Mechanical and Electrical Engineer, Scotland, was being seconded to the Ministry of Supply, as Director

12

2. ARP sandbagging outside the main offices in
Drummond Street.

of Transportation Equipment, and that he was
to take his place in Glasgow immediately. It was
all done in a shipwreck hurry. He was to meet
Riddles for breakfast at the Euston Hotel on the
following morning, see Fairburn for instruc-
tions at the wartime headquarters of the LMS at
The Grove, Watford, take the midday train to
Glasgow that same day, and that was that!

So, from those breathless moments of the first
week-end events gradually subsided into the
queer, uneasy period of the 'phoney war'. With
the rapid overthrow of Poland it was thought
that the strength of the German air force would
next be turned against Great Britain and France;

but this did not happen and the more unthinking
were lulled into a sense of security. There was
nothing phoney about the tasks set for the railways in that first winter, and the extent to which
travel facilities were curtailed and train services
decelerated was a measure of the seriousness
with which the situation was viewed. The
hampering conditions of working in the black-
out at night were, of course, not peculiar to the
LMS, and it was curious, in retrospect, to recall
the way in which the black-out was referred to
as an extenuating circumstance in the bad accident that occurred at Bletchley station on the
night of 13 October. The 7.50 pm Euston to
Stranraer, hauled by two engines, was being so
carelessly driven as to pass *six* successive adverse

13

3. Children being evacuated from London at the end of August 1939.

signals; and although booked to stop at Bletchley approached the station at such a speed as to come into violent collision with a shunting engine that was attaching vehicles to a preceding train. It was suggested that black-out conditions caused the driver of the leading engine of the express to lose his sense of locality, whereas, of course, the subduing of other lights actually made – or should have made! – the signals stand out that much more clearly.

A big resignalling scheme, which for security reasons was little known outside the railway service, was in progress at Crewe. The elaborate system of semaphores at the north and south ends of the passenger station was in process of replacement by colour lights: seventy-two of the new units, fitted where necessary with directional junction indicators, were to replace no fewer than 274 semaphore arms. After the trial of speed-signalling aspects at Mirfield, as described in volume 2 of this work, the signal engineer of the LMS, A. F. Bound, had reverted

14

to traditional British 'geographical' aspects, using directional junction indicators then coming into regular use on the LNER and the Southern. The new installation at Crewe was controlled from two new signal-boxes, massively built to ARP standards, with all-electric lever interlocking frames of the Westinghouse type. While nearly all the work was carried out in conditions of the closest security by LMS staff, Westinghouse erected the locking frames, as I well remember. During the course of the work, at a very 'jumpy' time in the war, I had occasion to go to Crewe and before

leaving a colleague who had been there previously said, 'Watch your step, or you might get a bayonet in your back!'

In the railway press the almost overnight deceleration of the passenger train service was sometimes the subject of faintly adverse comment, although due consideration was given to the circumstances of the time. So far as the LMS was concerned the timetables of October 1939 gave a generally slower service from London to provincial towns than that to which times had deteriorated after four years of the first world war. The following table shows the situation.

EMERGENCY MAIN LINE TIMETABLES: OCTOBER 1939
LONDON TO AND FROM PROVINCIAL CENTRES

London and	Distance Miles	Fastest Times			No. of Trains daily			Average Times		
		Oct 1918	Oct 1938	Oct 1939	Oct 1918	Oct 1938	Oct 1939	Oct 1918	Oct 1938	Oct 1939
		h m	h m	h m				h m	h m	h m
Leicester	99.1	2 15	1 39	2 31	18	30	16	2 33	1 48	2 46
Birmingham	112.9	2 40	1 55	2 41	11	20	15	2 53	2 05	3 10
Nottingham	123.5	2 55	2 03	3 06	12	21	12	3 07	2 25	3 31
Sheffield	158.5	4 01	2 56	4 25	12	20	10	4 24	3 12	4 44
Manchester	188.5	4 35	3 15	4 32	16	22	14	5 10	3 43	4 52
Liverpool	193.7	4 40	3 15	4 40	12	14	12	5 03	3 39	5 02
Leeds	196.0	4 47	3 48	5 35	12	16	8	5 25	4 06	6 03
Glasgow	401.4	9 30	6 30	9 35	6	12	6	10 20	8 06	10 04
Perth	450.4	10 10	8 41	11 12	6	8	4	11 19	9 30	11 31
Inverness	568.4	15 55	13 00	16 14	3	4	2	16 28	14 30	16 26

After their immediate and total withdrawal on the outbreak of war restaurant cars were re-instated on a number of trains, and in view of current prices it is amusing to recall the cost of the 'standard price' meals provided from 16 October onwards:

Standard breakfast, luncheon or dinner 2s 6d
Standard tea (when standard meal is
  available) 1s 0d
Sandwiches per round 1s 0d

From the outbreak of war the LMS staff journals *LMS Magazine*, *On Time* and *Quota News* were suspended. In their place a monthly newsletter entitled *Carry On* was produced and distributed gratuitously among the staff. The first issue included a message from Lord Stamp under the heading: 'Railways Vital to Nation's Cause: Whatever Befall, We Must Carry On'. He wrote:

It will ever be a source of pride to those

connected with the railways that when war did come it found us prepared to the last man and the last vehicle to play our part speedily, safely, and efficiently in the sudden special movements of traffic. We of the railways have the triple responsibility of war traffic movements, of maintaining essential food and other supplies, and of enabling the civil community to carry on. Knowing that we are fighting and working so that right and freedom may prevail there must be only one end. May we be able to say – as was said of the railways twenty years ago – that when the final victory is won, our share in it shall have been a worthy one.

The finer points of passenger rolling stock design faded into one of those pleasant pre-war conceptions regretfully put on the shelf, for the duration, when it became an urgent necessity to press into use any coaches that could run, and coaches that would hold the maximum number of passengers, sitting, standing, or lying, as was often to be the case in the luggage space of brake vans! But before the memory of it is confined to far-off things some reference must be made to the notable paper Stanier was to have read to the summer meeting of the Institution of Mechanical Engineers in New York, an abstract of which was subsequently published in the technical press. The desirability of restricting the weight of such stock is appreciated by all

4. ARP in the goods yard. Railwaymen in tin hats leaving a shelter in December 1939.

Fox Photos

5. The Bletchley collision on 14 October 1939. The 'Black
Five' no. 5025 in the foreground was the leading engine
of the express and the ex-LNW 0–8–0 was shunting in
the platform. No. 5025 is now preserved in working order
on the Strathspey Railway.

6. Poppy Day in wartime. The Euston stationmaster, still in top hat, placing a garland on the streamlined 4–6–2 no. 6224, 'Princess Alexandra', on Armistice Day 1939.

those who have to do with the running of trains, whether in the provision of motive power, in responsibility for track maintenance, or in handling the vehicles themselves in workshops. There is, of course, a limit in weight reduction beyond which it is unsafe to go; but by skilful design much can be achieved, and practice developed on the LMS up to 1939 had been noteworthy.

From a study of Stanier's paper it was evident that welding had played a highly significant part. Until the early 1930s the most usual form of main line coaching stock construction was to have a timber body framing built upon a steel underframe, but one of the most important early developments was to apply the technique of all-welded construction to the underframe and the bogie. By the use of edge-welded joints, instead of overlaps and riveting, a considerable saving in weight could be made. This was later developed into a girder type of underframe, in which each member was strong enough to carry its share of the load without the assistance of the others. The cross members were only spacers. The following table shows the effect of the two stages of development in welded construction of third-class corridor coaches.

Type	Riveted Standard	Welded 1st standard	Lightweight Welded
Wt. of complete vehicle tons	30.3	28.8	25.96
Tare weight per passenger, lb.	1,615	1,535	1,385

The introduction of much decelerated passenger train schedules, albeit with a general tendency to increase loads, emphasised the great value of having a large fleet of mixed traffic locomotives, with a high route availability and capable of operating over lengthy mileages with a minimum of intermediate servicing and atten-tion. The 'Black Five' 4–6–0, introduced in 1935, of which no fewer than 471 had been built up to 1938, had proved an extremely valuable investment. Although the first examples had medium degree superheaters, following the practice of the Great Western Railway, first adopted by Stanier, they did not suffer too badly compared with the 5X express passenger engines. But in later batches the 'Black Fives' were fitted with high degree superheaters, and showed greatly improved all-round per-formance. The three stages of boiler develop-ment were:

Stage	1	2	3
Superheater elements	14	24	28
Heating surfaces sq. ft			
Tubes	1,460	1,460	1,479
Firebox	156	171.3	171
Superheater	227.5	307.0	359
Total	1,843.5	1,938.3	2,009

Stage 3 refers to the batch built in 1938 at Crewe, and all subsequently. The class eventu-ally totalled no less than 842 locomotives.

2
Six Apocalyptic Months

In the first four months of war the British people as a whole had experienced little of what all-out war against Nazi Germany was going to involve. We had yet to learn the tactics that our principal enemy was to employ throughout the period that he was on the offensive, and several times during those first six months of 1940 it was supremely fortunate for Great Britain that he employed such a strategy. By the end of June the revelation of those tactics was not in the slightest doubt: it was, to deal with one thing, and one thing only, at a time. In the early months of the war the build-up of the British military position on the Continent was allowed to proceed unmolested, and when the extremely severe weather came after Christmas, and the transport services of this country were more seriously disrupted than at any time since the great storms of 1916, an opportunity to add grievously to our troubles by heavy bombing was let pass. It was not yet Britain's turn to be attacked.

From the railway viewpoint, and particularly that of the LMS, with its strategic lines to the far north of Scotland, the situation was grim — without any aggravation from the enemy. The full extent of the dislocation was, of course, not revealed until several weeks later, when normal working had been more or less restored; but those who were unfortunate enough to be travelling, or who were dependent upon the movements of others could form some idea of what was happening north of Crewe, when the arrival indicator at Euston had this cheerful information:

Train Due	From	Minutes late
4.17	Manchester, Stockport, Rugby	440
6.8	Liverpool, Crewe, Stafford, Rugby	200
—	Irish Mail: Holyhead, Chester, Crewe	270

Subjoined was a chalked up statement: 'No Scotch Trains Running'. While the whole country was seriously affected – even down in our wartime post in Wiltshire – the most severe dislocation was in a belt of country from the Derbyshire Peak District to Clydesdale. The Midland route to Manchester was completely blocked. The Settle and Carlisle had its usual quota of snow-blocks, but the worst of all so far as the LMS was concerned was on the north side of Beattock summit. Railway history had recorded nothing as severe as this. Emergency arrangements included the furnishing of railway buffets at the larger stations with additional supplies of food for passengers stranded in cancelled and disabled trains. Fortunately rationing of food had only just started and there were adequate supplies on hand.

7. Arctic weather – January 1940.

Several months later, when full statistics were available, it was learned that there were 238 separate snow-blocks, which between them affected 1,056 route miles of track. A total of seventy-one trains were completely blocked in by snow drifts and of these in only fifteen cases were the locomotives able to 'escape', to try and get help. Three expresses which had left Glasgow Central for the south on the morning of 28 January were brought to a stand near Beattock summit, and in the deepening drifts virtually buried. Many of the passengers were not able to proceed for five days. Even in the level country south of Lancaster the shallow cuttings quickly filled with snow, and between Brock and Garstang one block was not cleared for four days. In that location snow-ploughs could not be used, because of the presence of

21

water troughs. No Anglo-Scottish expresses by either route ran between the night of 27 January and 2 February. On the Settle and Carlisle one of the worst blocks was near Aisgill summit. The line between Skipton and Colne was completely blocked for the whole period of the worst weather. Strangely enough the Highland section, normally the most severely affected of all, was not mentioned in the official communiqués that were issued subsequently. When the worst of it was over the Railway Executive Committee displayed a poster, thus:

CENSORED

In peace-time railways could explain
When fog or ice held up your train

But now the country's waging war
To tell you why's against the law

The censor says you must not know
When there's been a fall of snow

That's because it would be *news*
The Germans could not fail to *use*

So think of this, if it's your fate
To have to meet a train that's late

Railways aren't allowed to say
What delayed the trains today

Actually the exceptionally severe weather was general all over western and north western Europe, and from information that came our way it seemed that Germany was one of the hardest hit countries of all!

On 5 March there was an alarming accident on the steeply graded section of the Highland main line between Aviemore and Slochd summit. Its very occurrence, however, was enough to show how remarkably free this difficult

section of railway had always been from serious accidents, having regard particularly to the hazards involved in working heavy unbraked freight trains over such steep gradients. A heavy loaded mineral train consisting of thirty wagons and a 20-ton brake van, weighing 460 tons, was taken from Aviemore up to Slochd by two Stanier 'Black Five' 4–6–0s, but on approaching Slochd the train was stopped at the home signal, afterwards being drawn into the down loop line. On arrival in the loop it was found that only nine wagons were attached to the two engines. The two drivers were unaware of the break-away, because of a broken wrought iron drawbar hook, and that twenty-one wagons and the brake van were running away on a 1 in 70 gradient. The guard soon realised he could not control them and jumped sustaining injuries, but in view of what happened afterwards undoubtedly saving his life.

The signalman at Slochd, having conferred with the two drivers, did not at first seem to realise that the rest of the train was still not standing where it had first stopped; but when he did, and telephoned Carr Bridge, 5½ miles away, it was too late. On a gradient that had steepened to 1 in 60 the runaway had already attained a high speed, and the signalman at Carr Bridge could only watch it dash through and send the 'Obstruction Danger' signal to Aviemore. Again he was just too late to prevent the dispatch of another northbound freight train, also double-headed. About 2½ miles north of Aviemore they saw red lights, and before there was time to do anything the runaway crashed head-on into them. The pilot engine was turned over and its crew killed, and such was the violence of the collision that fourteen out of the twenty-one vehicles of the runaway together with the brake van were destroyed. While the primary cause of the accident was due to the breaking of the drawbar

8. The terrible traffic hold ups of January 1940, with the arrival board at Euston showing trains up to 440 minutes late.

hook, the dire consequences emphasise the need for great vigilance in working loose-coupled freight trains over such severe gradients.

On 11 March, anticipating by one month the German invasion of Norway, the War Office declared a large area in the north of Scotland a protected area. This included the whole of the counties of Caithness, Sutherland, and Ross and Cromarty, and all those parts of Inverness-shire and Argyll lying west of the Great Glen. The only part excepted was the Burgh of Inverness.

This included the whole of the Farther North section of the old Highland Railway, together with the Dingwall and Skye line. From that time onwards no one other than residents, those who had official passes, or who were members of the armed forces of the Crown was allowed to enter the area. It included, of course, all the Inner and Outer Hebrides, and although not directly concerning the LMS, the Mallaig extension of the West Highland line. The invasion of Denmark and Norway came on 19 April, and introduced a long, hostile coastline on the opposite side of the North Sea; otherwise the build-up of the

23

9. A characteristic wartime scene at St Pancras, with sunshine through the open roof highlighting the otherwise prevailing gloom.

10. An ARP 'strongpoint' at Bletchley, surmounting an emergency control post.

British Expeditionary Force behind the French frontier with the Low Countries still went on, with no sign of any major hostilities developing.

In view of the violence of the storm that was so soon to break it is astonishing in retrospect to find *The Railway Gazette*, as late as 3 May 1940, reviewing 'Holidays by LMS', thus:

> Notwithstanding the war, the L.M.S.R. has had a keen demand and extensive advertising support for its holiday guide for England and Wales. The latest edition comprises 684 pages, of which 100 are devoted to photographs reproduced in gravure. More than 300 resorts in the diverse holiday districts served by the line are described. It is an excellent sixpenny-worth. As usual, a separate 'Scottish Holiday Guide' is also published.

Nor was the LMS alone. The other three main line companies were prompt with their usual holiday publications. Even Cooks, in compliance with the government request that reciprocal travel between England and France should not be discouraged, had planned a few inclusive holidays in Paris and other parts of France. Exactly a week later, in the early hours of Friday 10 May, the blitzkrieg started in earnest, with the invasion of Holland, Belgium, and Luxembourg. It was the Whitsun holiday weekend. With government approval the railways had a programme of extra trains for holidaymakers; but these, and the Whit Monday holiday were summarily cancelled. How quickly and catastrophically the military situation on the Continent deteriorated is a matter of history; but one intended LMS contribution to the transportation equipment of the BEF, too

25

11. Inside the emergency control post at Bletchley, showing track diagrams and telephone equipment.

late to take any part in the campaigns of 1940, must be specially mentioned.

On the outbreak of war a number of ex-GCR 2–8–0 freight locomotives (LNER Class 04), which had seen service with the ROD in the First World War, were adapted for service in France with the BEF; but it was estimated that many more locomotives would be required, and in December 1939 the Ministry of Supply ordered a further 240 of the 2–8–0 type. R. A. Riddles, as Director of Transportation Equipment at the Ministry of Supply, specified the Stanier 8F type of the LMS for this order, but including a number of modifications, for wartime service behind the lines. To some, whose preferences as locomotive enthusiasts lie elsewhere, this choice of an LMS design for national

service might savour slightly of prejudice; but actually it was from all-round considerations the best that was then readily available. The Great Western 2–8–0, like that of the former Great Central, had Stephenson's link motion inside, necessitating a pit for attention, while the Gresley 3-cylinder design of the LNER, with its conjugated valve gear, was too much of a 'Rolls Royce' for service behind a battle front. In any case the LMS 8F was considerably modified in detail to render it suitable for service on the French railways. The brake was Westinghouse, instead of vacuum; water pick-up gear was omitted, though it did seem that a Flaman type self-recording speed indicator was a somewhat unnecessary luxury. Delivery was taken of the first of these locomotives on 24 May, but in view of the rapidly worsening situation on the Continent none of them crossed the Channel.

12. One of the standard LMS corridor 'brake third' coaches of 1930 converted into an ambulance car at Swindon Works.

H. C. Casserley Collection

Use was eventually found for them in Egypt and the Middle East.

The tactics of the enemy in concentrating on one thing at a time were never more vividly and providentially shown than at the time of the Dunkirk evacuation. However much the retreating armies were strafed on Continental soil, and while embarking on the beaches, the harassment was not continued at the English ports of disembarkation, and the dispersal of no less than 320,000 men proceeded without any interruption. The LMS share in that historic operation was the provision of forty-four trains, which shuttled back and forth as required; and while it was, of course, the Southern that had by far the heaviest task in getting the men away from the Channel ports, there was then quite frequently no clear idea of where the trains would eventually be routed. There were no working notices; the whole operation was organised entirely by telephone, and when it is recalled that some trains conveyed the survivors as far north as Aberdeen, it will be appreciated that the British

genius for improvisation was strained almost to the limit.

The alarming development by the enemy, during the campaign in France and the Low Countries, of dropping parachutists in the rear of the battle line had led to the formation of the Local Defence Volunteers. At first railwaymen, who already had duties in connection with Air Raid Precautions, were dissuaded from joining; but very soon, with most other spare time activities put on one side 'for the duration', LMS men, in common with the men of other railways, were permitted to take this additional voluntary duty. When, in July, the title of this force, hitherto the Local Defence Volunteers (LDV), was changed to Home Guard, the LMS set the seal on the occasion by the ceremonial naming at Euston of one of the Baby Scot class of 4–6–0 express locomotives, no. 5543 'Home Guard'. It was on Tuesday 30 July that Lt-Gen. Sir Henry Pownall, Inspector General of the Home Guard, performed the ceremony, and in introducing the general Lord Stamp said that no less than 50,000 of the company's staff had enrolled in the Home Guard.

3
The Night Blitz of 1940–41

The Nazi attempt to knock out the fighter-plane stations of the RAF as a preliminary to full-scale invasion, during the ever-memorable Battle of Britain, did not affect the LMS to any serious extent; but when this failed and the enemy switched his tactics to the night bombing of London, and then to many provincial centres it was a very different story. In addition to the London area there were severe attacks on Coventry, Liverpool, Manchester, Derby, Clydeside and Belfast, in all of which LMS activities suffered badly. The Irish Sea and its ports, together with the Firth of Clyde, became the reception area for the ocean-going convoys that constituted the great national lifeline. In the winter of 1940/1 it was mainly a question of food and fuel but from 1941, after the celebrated Atlantic Meeting between Winston Churchill and President Roosevelt, it became the supply route under the Lend-Lease arrangement.

Before bombing started in earnest the regulations regarding the running of trains during air raids were restrictive. Signalmen were required to stop trains entering an area under a red alert, to warn drivers, and the ordinary headlamp code had then to be changed to one of a single lamp, to indicate that the driver had been notified. The maximum speed of passenger trains had then to be 15 mph; subsequently

increased to 25 mph. But in the early autumn of 1940, when the additional purple warning was introduced to indicate confidentially to railways and industrial premises that raiders were about, but that an attack did not seem imminent, traffic was permitted to run normally, though all external lighting had naturally to be extinguished. Actually the drivers came to pay little attention even to red alerts, even when the sirens were sounded. I have vivid recollections of a late evening journey north from Bristol at the end of September 1940 and hearing the sirens sounding about one hour after we had started; but we continued at full speed, sometimes touching 70 mph. Just where we ran out of the 'alert' area I do not know, but on reaching our destination in the north Midlands we found they were still under a purple warning, with all railway lights out in an adjoining marshalling yard.

In that first winter it seemed that the tactics of the enemy were directed more towards intimidating the morale of the civilian population by high-level, non-precision bombing rather than by systematic attacks on targets, the destruction of which would cause serious embarrassment to war production. Even so the damage was extensive enough, except to the morale of the people. There was no waiting for the 'all-clear' to sound before repair gangs went out, and the restoration of services was in-

13. A 'roof spotter' on the look out for enemy aircraft above Camden locomotive running shed on 29 November 1940. The engine below is 4–6–2 no. 6211, 'Queen Maud'.

Fox Photos

credibly rapid. It was fortunate beyond measure that the many alternative routes remaining from the time of unbridled competition between one-time individual companies were still available for temporary diversions. The lean years of the early 1930s, when so much was done to reduce expenditure, had not progressed to the extent of closing many alternative routes and lifting the track. Nevertheless, there were times, as at Coventry in November 1940 and Liverpool in May 1941, when *every* possible route was damaged. But these situations could, through the resolution and, indeed, heroism of the repair gangs, be reckoned in hours rather than days. There were, of course, spectacular incidents like the direct hit on St Pancras; but even this did not at any time interrupt the flow of traffic into and out of the station, intricate though the tasks were for the men of the Chief Civil Engineer's department in making first temporary, and then permanent restoration of the damaged platforms.

The damage at St Pancras, caused by five bombs that fell during the raid on 10 May, was complicated by the construction of the station itself, with the platforms in the roof, as it were. One 1,000-lb. bomb went clean through the station floor – which consisted of wrought iron plates on wrought iron main and cross-girders, resting on cast iron columns – clean through the basement below, and exploded about 25 feet down in the solid clay. Although the blast from this naturally affected the station floor and formed a large crater at the concourse end of platforms 3 and 4, the whole process of repair was much complicated by the actual explosion occurring behind the side wall of the tunnel from the Metropolitan line, over which Midland trains run to Moorgate, over the City Widened Lines. The tunnel lining was destroyed for a length of about 20 feet and the tunnel itself completely blocked with debris.

An immediate examination of all the cast iron columns supporting the station floor showed which were unsafe, and the floor area concerned was barricaded off to enable traffic to be resumed in the unaffected parts of the station. Clearing up the mess below was hindered because there was an unexploded bomb further up No. 2 platform. Until this had been removed the girders, plates and damaged coaches overhanging the main crater could not be cleared away, and a ballast train drawn into the Metropolitan tunnel could not proceed very far, to start on the removal of the debris. In view of all that was involved it was remarkable that traffic was resumed on all lines, except for two platforms, only seven days after this major incident.

The concentrated attack on Coventry on the night of 14/15 November was one of the worst

Great Britain suffered during the whole of the war; in fact, the number of incidents on the railways around the city was nearly double that experienced in any one night anywhere else on the LMS – no fewer than 122! Every line through Coventry was blocked. Traffic between Euston and Birmingham was diverted at Rugby, making a long detour via Leamington, Kenilworth and back onto the main line at Berkswell. However, within two days repairs at Coventry station enabled one platform to be reopened and normal service resumed on the main line between London and Birmingham. The line between Brandon and Three Spires Junction was very important as an alternative, between Rugby and Nuneaton, to the Trent Valley main line, and although lying somewhat outside the city area no fewer than forty-three incidents were reported over its length of 3½ miles. This was, incidentally, a commentary upon the inaccuracy of the Nazi bombing, seeing that so much high explosive was unloaded well outside the principal target area. The tally of death and destruction in the city itself was, however, grievous enough. It was not until a week after the raid that the avoiding line was reopened for traffic. Although the repair gangs worked simultaneously, from both ends, they could not gain access to the more seriously damaged parts of the line until the effects of lesser incidents had been patched up sufficiently to allow work trains to proceed.

The effectiveness of measures taken for protecting the vital centres of control were illustrated, in part, by two major incidents, one in Manchester and one in Belfast. The Control Centres of the Central Division (former LYR lines) was in Manchester, and an emergency room, 30 feet below ground level, was in use when the Luftwaffe launched a heavy attack just before Christmas 1940. All was going well, until water began to pour in. A nearby reservoir

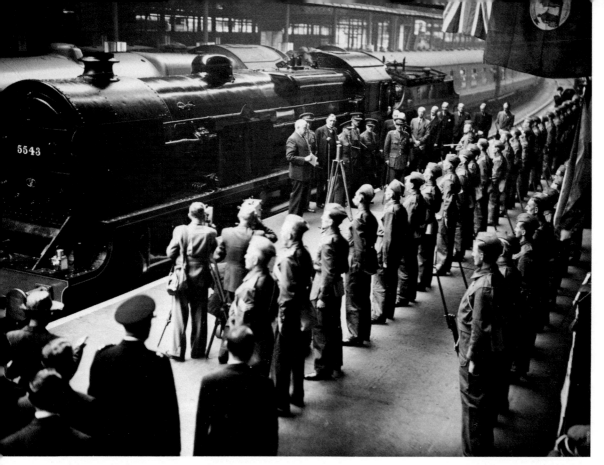

14. Wartime naming ceremony at Euston on 30 July 1940. Patriot class 4–6–0 no. 5543 is named 'Home Guard' by Lt-Gen. Sir Henry Pownall, Inspector General of the Home Guard.

had been breached and water was cascading down. The staff had perforce to evacuate, and for a time, with even the emergency control out of action and many telephone and signal wires damaged, the Central Division was operated by improvisation and by the conveyance of orders by car and motor-cycle dispatch riders to the strategic points. In Belfast the intrepid Major M. S. Speir had, in 1938, insisted on building air raid shelters and strengthening the signal-box, when most people felt that Northern Ireland would be largely immune from enemy attack.

How wise he was! The Luftwaffe struck early in April 1941, and although the General Stores, the Parcels Office, the Audit Office and the Engineer's Drawing Office were destroyed, the signal-box and its delicate equipment withstood the worst the bombs could do, thanks to the brick reinforcement of the walls and the steel roof. On 4 May 1941 there was a terrible raid on Belfast in which the NCC lost twenty passenger coaches and 270 freight wagons, but again Control and communications were no more than slightly affected.

The most severe test to which the resources of the LMS were subjected was in the Liverpool area in May 1941, when for seven consecutive

15. Coventry station soon after the terrible night raid of 14–15 November 1940.

National Railway Museum

nights heavy attacks were launched. Twice during that fearful week every railway exit from Liverpool was blocked in some way. Fires raged continuously, the water supply was frequently exhausted or interrupted by more bomb damage, and there were times when only the emergency bus services kept Liverpool going. They provided means of continuity between points over which railway lines were destroyed; they got the repair gangs to the job, even though at one time no fewer than 500 parallel roads were obstructed. It was sometimes said during the blitz that if one centre had more than three consecutive nights of heavy raiding it would bring morale near to breaking point. Liverpool had *seven*, and still managed to carry on. There was no question of who the lines belonged to when alternative routeing was needed; on the Liverpool side of the Mersey estuary the LMS and the Cheshire Lines were all one in May 1941.

16. The scene on the morning after the raid on St Pancras, 10 May 1941.

Many LMS men and women were killed while on duty but the crowning misfortune for the Company, and for the British railways in general, came on the night of 17 April 1941 when Lord Stamp, his wife and eldest son were killed during the destruction of their home in Beckenham as a result of a direct hit. His loss was irreparable. Aged, then, no more than sixty-one, he was in the very prime of his life, and one can only imagine of what immense value his experience and service would have been in the difficult years after the war. As recorded in the first volume of this book he became the first President of the Executive of the LMS in 1926, and in the autumn of 1927, having in the meantime been elected a director of the Company, he succeeded Sir Guy Granet as Chairman. Thereafter, most skilfully and successfully he combined the two offices. It was due to Granet that he was wooed away from his very important post as Director and Secretary

17. How the damage was patched up at St Pancras, and the platforms affected made usable again. A picture taken in August 1942.

of Nobel Industries Ltd, later one of the most important constituents of Imperial Chemical Industries. At the time of his death Granet wrote:

> He was a rare and endearing personality. His mental equipment was pre-eminent and was always at the service of the company to its

great benefit, the extent of which has not yet been realised. But it was the sweetness and nobility of his character, his accessibility, his capacity for work, and his almost uncanny power of understanding what was in a man and his power of drawing it out of him, that impressed me more than anything as a manager, and organiser, and leader.

The serenity of his temper and his ever present sense of humour made all the wheels of the machine work more sweetly and easily.

18. Night express in a bomb crater. A bomb landed on the line at Queens Park just before the 7.20 pm express from Euston approached. The engine fell into the hole and the train was derailed.

A week after the death of Lord Stamp the Board of the LMS met and appointed Sir Thomas Royden, Bart, as Chairman, though not combining the duties of President of the Executive. The new Chairman had an almost lifelong connection with railways, having as long previously as 1909 been made a Director of the Lancashire and Yorkshire Railway. On the amalgamation with the LNWR in 1922 he became a director of the enlarged Company, and of the LMS, on Grouping. In 1940 he had been elected a Deputy Chairman. At the time of Lord Stamp's death the four Vice-Presidents of the LMS were Sir William Wood (who represented the LMS on the wartime Railway Executive Committee), Sir Harold Hartley, Sir Ernest Lemon and Mr Ashton Davies, and Sir William Wood was chosen as the new President of the Executive. Only a month after the death of Lord Stamp another great personality of the LMS group of companies died, but in less violent circumstances. This was Sir Thomas Williams, the former General Manager of the London and North Western Railway, before the amalgamation with the LYR. Sir Thomas died at his home at St Margaret's-on-Thames in his 89th year. He was a Director of the LMS until 1939.

Reverting to the blitz, it is remarkable to recall in those strained and anxious times how many eminent men came forward to undertake duties which in peacetime would have seemed onerous enough in addition to their ordinary duties; and it was in the early spring of 1941, of all years, that Mr W. A. Stanier became President of the Institution of Mechanical Engineers, and inaugurated a year that was notable for the exceptionally high quality of its technical papers – blitz, or no blitz!

4
The Works at War

By the early months of 1940 all the railway works throughout the country were being urged to undertake a maximum amount of war production; and those of the LMS were soon involved in some very unusual tasks. Crewe, under the able management of the ex-LNW veteran F. A. Lemon, had taken on anything and everything it was offered; but a very unusual assignment came to CME headquarters at Derby. Under the supervision of H. G. Ivatt, who was then Principal Assistant (Locomotives), full responsibility was taken for the design of the new Mark V cruiser tanks, the Covenanters, and a section of the drawing office under J. W. Caldwell was set aside for this special duty. It was no small achievement for a group of men, hitherto specialists in steam locomotives, to undertake, with complete success, the design of an armoured fighting machine. Caldwell himself later became chief draughtsman of the LMS. Manufacture of the Covenanters was allocated to Crewe amongst other works with a delivery requirement of four per week, from Crewe itself.

Nevertheless, it went almost without saying that the repair of locomotives remained a vital task at all the main works. With capacity for new construction largely absorbed by special wartime tasks the 'scrap and build' programme, replacing obsolescent types by the new Stanier standards, had perforce to be halted. The maintenance in good shape of the Bowen Cooke superheater 0–8–0s of Class G1, of which there were still more than a hundred in service, was an important instance. Scrapping of other older types virtually ceased. Furthermore, pre-war plans for the rationalisation of manufacturing facilities including the closing or contraction of certain sections of various works were all halted. Even though shops might not be used to the fullest advantage space had to be kept in hand as a precaution against major damage from air attack. This was particularly the case in Scotland. Lying in a densely populated industrial area the former Caledonian works at St Rollox, near also to the great establishments of the North British Locomotive Company, seemed to be particularly vulnerable; accordingly some space and reserved capacity at Kilmarnock was considered essential.

In Scotland an unusual and vital use was made of the former Glasgow and South Western works at Barassie which had become a major wagon works for the Northern Division – a government contract was negotiated for the repair of Spitfire aircraft. While the carriage shops at the great English works of Wolverton and Derby established production lines for manufacture and repair of wings for the Hampden and Lancaster bombers, Barassie

British Rail

19. A Covenanter tank, of which 161 were built at Crewe.

undertook the complete repair of damaged aircraft, even to the extent of building an airstrip from which those invaluable fighters could fly away under their own power after repair. The airstrip was constructed on an adjoining golf-course requisitioned for the purpose and two hangars were built in which final assembly of the reconditioned aircraft was carried out. The production and inspection staff on Spitfires at one time numbered about 500, half of which were women.

In 1941 Crewe had been set a target output of four Covenanter tanks a week, plus forty repaired locomotives. It was hoped that new locomotives at a rate of three per fortnight would be outshopped but in actual fact, except for repaired locomotives, the programme was running somewhat in arrears, largely because

the back-up services had not expanded to an appropriate extent. Repaired locomotives were coming off the celebrated belt system after a stay of no more than six to eight days for a complete heavy repair. Even this was a little longer than the time envisaged when the system was first installed by H. P. M. Beames, mainly because the locomotives being dealt with were generally larger and more complicated – even though more thermally efficient. When the system was first installed, except for the Claughtons, there were few other than ex-LNW standard types, and these had inside cylinders with Joy valve gears. In 1941 the repairs, not necessarily all 'heavy generals', included 54 to Pacifics, 119 to Royal Scots, 193 to Jubilees and Baby Scots, and 38 to the Midland Division Garratts all of which were maintained at Crewe.

20. Horwich Works with an assembly line of Matilda
tanks, the hull plates of which were machined at Crewe.

It was in this critical year of 1941 that Stanier
decided the time had come for a change in the
works management at Crewe. F. A. Lemon, a
premium apprentice and pupil under F. W.
Webb, and who had served under eight Chief
Mechanical Engineers, had been in the chair
since 1920, designated first as Works Manager
and then from 1931 Works Superintendent.
A North Western man by training, and un-
shakably loyal to successive generations of high
management, he had a quiet charm and courtesy
of manner that I well remember. For one of my
very early literary assignments I was privileged
to visit Crewe at the time the second batch

of Princess Royal class Pacifics was on the
assembly line, and I saw nos 6208, 6209 and
6210 in successive stages of construction. I
shall never forget how Lemon received me
personally, and spoke quietly and enthusiasti-
cally of the great changes being wrought in
the locomotive department of the LMS under
Stanier. That was in the summer of 1935.
To succeed Lemon Stanier brought R. C.
Bond down from Glasgow, another felicitous
appointment, particularly as he knew the works
well from his previous appointment as Assistant
Works Superintendent from 1933 to 1937.

He took over at a critical time in the war.
Having failed signally in the various aerial

21. Barassie Works (ex-G&SWR) with damaged fuselages of Spitfire aircraft being repaired.

attacks on this country, albeit inflicting grievous damage upon many industrial centres and port facilities, Hitler had flung the German army against Russia, and in the welcome respite Winston Churchill had crossed the Atlantic to the historic meeting with President Roosevelt to negotiate the invaluable arrangements for obtaining all kinds of war equipment. In the meantime Crewe, to its own amazement, had remained almost entirely immune from air attack and the constant efforts to increase production continued, even though 300 men had been loaned to Rolls Royce for stepping up the production of Merlin engines for fighter aircraft. In the works itself there were by that time

no fewer than 1,000 women employed, many on jobs previously considered exclusive to skilled tradesmen, while heftier damsels drove drop stamps and heavy steam hammers.

As the war progressed, and the demands on heavy industry were modified by the arrival of much additional equipment from across the Atlantic, the urgent need for new locomotives became evident. At Crewe the situation was simple enough: it was tanks, or locomotives; one could not have both. There was a limit to the extent to which old locomotives could be patched up and made serviceable. When the 'scrap and build' programme had reached its full intensity in the years 1935–7 Crewe was scrapping on an average about 220 locomotives a

22. Derby Works with aircraft assembly on a large scale.

year. In 1941 only ten were scrapped; and when it is recalled that engines being maintained included Webb 17-inch coal 0–6–0s and many 18-inch 'Cauliflowers', it will be appreciated that the Motive Power Department was being extended to a critical degree. The situation at Crewe certainly had its counterparts at Derby, Horwich and St Rollox.

The question of locomotive repairs was assuming a new and crucial phase. On all counts there was an urgent need to get increased monthly mileages from engines, and although the actual work on the road was not generally so demanding as on the fast pre-war schedules the loads were much heavier, the fuel less carefully graded, and attention to locomotives on shed somewhat attenuated at times. There was a tendency for the Motive Power Department to send for shopping units that were still serviceable, and to hold back others that had been 'stopped'; and it was found essential to even out the situation between the Western, Midland, Central and Northern Divisions by frequent telephone check-ups, to ensure that repair work was programmed to the best advantage of the railway as a whole.

W. Hubert Foster – author's collection

23. A wartime locomotive development. One of the first
of the converted Royal Scot class 4–6–0s no. 6117,
'Welsh Guardsman', working a St Pancras–Glasgow
express near Bell Busk.

24. A secret task completed. A very impressive load of 12-inch rail-mounted howitzers, built by the LMS, leaving for service in France in December 1944.

With increasing age the cracking of loco-motive frames was becoming a matter of grow-ing concern. Furthermore, it was not only the older engines that were victims to this malady; a disturbing proportion of the 'Black-Five' 4–6–0s was also involved. One curious anomaly, or so it seemed to those responsible, was that the 5X 4–6–0s were remarkably free from trouble whereas the Royal Scots were not; yet both had an almost identical frame design. Frames or not, as the war progressed the Baby Scots, if not the Jubilees, gradually acquired a shocking reputation among the enginemen. I shall always remember a very intelligent Scots fireman from Polmadie shed stigmatising the Baby Scots as the 'wur-r-rld's wur-rst'! As it transpired I never had an oppor-tunity of riding on the footplate of one of them; but I do not think they can have been more uncomfortable than one or two of the high-

mileage 'Black Fives' I sampled just after the war.

The incidence of frame fractures and the time it took to repair them tended to delay the general repair turn-round time, which was normally maintained at six to eight days, to something like a fortnight, and at Crewe the proposition was made that they should have spare frames available in the same way as a stock of spare boilers was always on hand. But the frame was basically the locomotive itself, and the suggestion was tantamount to seeking authority to build additional locomotives. However, in view of the urgency in maintaining the output of repaired locomotives the construction of three spare frames was authorised, one each for the three most standard types then going through the works, namely the Midland Class 4 0–6–0, the LNW G1 class 0–8–0, and the 'Black Five'. This modest concession, though a mere bagatelle compared to the regular provision of spare boilers, proved a great help.

Although little time could be spared for any-thing in the way of new locomotive design, in

1942 consideration was given to the provision of a larger version of the standard taper boiler on the Jubilee class 3-cylinder 4–6–0s. This had been prompted by the success of the boiler fitted in 1938 to the rebuild of the high-pressure compound 4–6–0 'Fury', as an additional engine of the Royal Scot class, no. 6170, named 'British Legion'. This engine had a boiler designed on Stanier principles together with a twin-orifice blastpipe and double chimney. It was a modified version of this boiler that was put onto two Jubilee class 4–6–0s, nos. 5735 and 5736. This was followed by the virtual renewal of ten of the Royal Scots, fitted with the same boiler. Although classified as rebuilds these latter were virtually new engines. They had new frames and new cylinders, a bolster bogie and modified spring gear, while a front-end in the Stanier style with a circular smokebox resting on a cast saddle eliminated some of the troubles experienced on the original Scots, which had the Derby type of built-up smokebox and mounting. Four of the new engines nos. 6103, 6108, 6109 and 6117 were allocated to Leeds (Midland) shed, and were put onto the double-home turns worked between Leeds and Glasgow St Enoch. They soon came into the limelight in 'British Locomotive Practice and Performance' in *The Railway Magazine*, as will be told in the next chapter.

In connection with some writing I was doing for *The Engineer* newspaper I had some interesting correspondence with Mr Ivatt about these locomotives. He sent me copies of indicator diagrams that had been taken on some running trials, and I was interested to see that the engine in question, no. 6138, had been worked at the same very short cut-offs that were customary on the 2300 class 2–6–4 tanks on the Euston–Watford–Tring suburban trains, and which were used on the 2–6–0s of the NCC in Ireland. But while the diagrams taken from no. 6138

Converted Royal Scot Engine No. 6138

Cut-off per cent	Speed mph	Indicated horsepower
5	62	925
10	60	1070
15	60	1520
18	62	1670
22	56	1700
26	52	1820
32	44	1840
38	30	1670
46	22	1440
Full gear	5	420

showed very high indicated horsepower in relation to the cut-offs used, I had come to appreciate that a very short cut-off did not in itself represent an exceptional thermal efficiency, but rather a characteristic of the valve setting. It was later shown that the taper-boilered Scots were little different in thermal efficiency from other British express passenger locomotives of comparable tractive power, for example the Great Western Castles and the Gresley A3 Pacifics. This is, however, drawing rather ahead of the period of this particular chapter.

It was in the later stages of the war that important changes took place in the Chief Mechanical Engineer's department. Stanier's towering status in the engineering world, and his vast practical experience made his services sought after in the highest government circles, and the day to day running of his great department on the LMS devolved almost entirely on Fairburn, even more so from 1943 when Stanier was appointed one of three scientific advisers to the Ministry of Production. In 1944 he retired from railway service and was succeeded as CME by Fairburn. The organisation of the department remained unchanged. No deputy was appointed and the principal assistants continued in their respective spheres.

5
Express Train Running, 1940–44

In a war such as we were waging, with the United Kingdom first of all an isolated bastion of defence against the forces that had overrun practically the whole of western Europe, and then the assembly ground and springboard for the Allied re-entry into Europe, one could not expect the standards of main line express running to which we had previously been accustomed on the LMS, and on all other lines for that matter, to be sustained. The drastic deceleration of all train times was an acknowledgment of this situation. The advertised passenger train services no longer had first priority. Government traffic was accorded preference when any cases of urgency arose. It is true that the wartime schedules in themselves were very much slower than those previously operating, and would have been easy enough to achieve even with the very heavy trains frequently operated. But with a vastly increased volume of freight traffic, and numerous special trains for naval and military personnel, signal checks were frequent. All this is quite apart from the exceptional delays and diversions arising from air raid damage on the line, or sudden changes in operating programmes on account of shipping movements. This was to have a special effect on LMS work-

ing north of Crewe, when the American forces began to arrive and the transatlantic convoys might be switched from one port of disembarkation to another at very short notice.

After the drastic initial limitation of speed to a maximum of 60 mph, this was relaxed over the principal routes of the LMS to 75 mph at the same time as an exhortation to drivers to use the capacity of their locomotives for making up lost time wherever possible. As always on the railways of Britain there were wide differences in the way individual drivers interpreted the last mentioned directive; some made little attempt to improve on the wartime point-to-point allowance, while others ran almost up to pre-war standards of performance when such was required for regaining lost time. Nevertheless, an observer taking details from some seat (or stance!) in the train would not necessarily be aware of extenuating conditions on the footplate; and at the shed locomotives did not have the careful attention that was usually given, in pre-war years, especially to those rostered for long through workings. Quite a number of London–Glasgow through runs were operated with the engines being remanned at Crewe or Carlisle en route.

The day Anglo-Scottish expresses were

W. Philip Conolly

25. In typical wartime condition, the streamlined Pacific no. 6243, 'City of Lancaster', entering Crewe with a southbound express.

allowed 182 minutes for the 141 miles from Crewe to Carlisle, in the proportion of 66 minutes to Preston (51 miles), 33 minutes on to Carnforth (27.3 miles) and 49 minutes for the 31.4 miles up to Shap summit. On one trip, with a fifteen-coach train making a gross trailing load of 500 tons, one of the non-streamlined engines of the Princess-Coronation class (later more familiarly known as the Duchesses) was delayed so as to take 73 minutes to pass Preston; but although the engine was in good condition

and steaming freely the driver did no more than keep sectional time onwards to Carlisle. The time over the mountain section from Carnforth to Shap summit was 47¾ minutes. The minimum speeds were 27 mph on Grayrigg bank and 19¼ mph at the summit. On another occasion, however, with one of the streamlined engines and a load of 475 tons, with the train leaving Crewe 15 minutes late, so resolute an attempt was made to regain lost time that had it not been for a signal stop outside the Citadel station, Carlisle would have been reached slightly ahead of time. On this occasion, after having taken

45

W. Philip Conolly

26. Up Anglo-Scottish express passing Lancaster, hauled by 4–6–2 no. 6234, 'Duchess of Abercorn'. This photograph, and also that on page 51, though typical of wartime, show the deflecting shields fitted to the Duchess class 4–6–2s after the 1945 accident at Ecclefechan.

64¼ minutes to pass Preston and despite three signal checks, the next 85¼ miles, over Shap, were covered in 94½ minutes. Allowing for the signal checks the net running time from Crewe to Carlisle was no more than 157 minutes – 25 minutes inside schedule.

The section of line between Preston and Carlisle, when free of signal checks and other hindrances, was the scene of much very fine running with these heavy and crowded wartime trains, and details of the last mentioned trip, made early in 1941, may be set alongside two others made in 1942 with still heavier loads, when the performance of the Stanier Pacific engines over this section was fully up to pre-war standards. In all three cases the engine was working through from Euston to Glasgow. The speeds at the critical points in the journey have been set out at the foot of the table of running times.

Run no.		1	2	3
Engine 4–6–2 no.		6237	6221	6234
Load tons E/F		445/475	480/525	499/560

Dist Miles		Sch min	Actual m s	Actual m s	Actual m s
0.0	PRESTON	0	0 00	0 00	0 00
—			—	—	p.w & sigs
21.0	Lancaster	26	23 32	24 27	26 32
27.3	Carnforth	33	29 30	30 15	32 03
40.1	Oxenholme	50	43 06	43 23	46 25
47.2	Grayrigg		54 13	53 18	57 04
53.2	Tebay	69	60 54	59 41	62 33
58.7	Shap summit	81	70 04	67 54	72 10
72.2	Penrith	96	83 06	80 51	85 23
—			sigs	sigs	—
90.1	CARLISLE	116	105 44	102 42	102 23
Net running time (min.)			100	96	98½

	mph	mph	mph
Max. before Carnforth	69	74	71½
Min. Grayrigg summit	31	37	35½
Max. at Tebay	68	67	67
Min. Shap summit	31	30	22½
Max. down to Carlisle	77½	79	80½

The times over the uphill section of 31.4 miles from Carnforth to Shap summit call for special mention, being 40 minutes 34 seconds, 37 minutes 39 seconds, and 40 minutes 7 seconds, representing average speeds of 46.4, 50, and 47 mph with these heavy trains, in which time the trains had negotiated a vertical rise of 885 feet, an average gradient of 1 in 185. Quite apart from the technical quality of the performance, which was high, these runs afforded notable examples of drivers and fireman 'going to it' – to quote the wartime slogan – to recover lost time.

An Anglo-Scottish service that came to create a good deal of public interest at the time was the briefly celebrated 'Ghost Train', running nightly in each direction between Euston and Glasgow St Enoch. A perspicacious observer at Euston one night saw a heavy and crowded train leaving that was not in the timetable. Patriotic, and having endured the restrictions imposed by the government on the running of extra trains he was curious, and by further observation found that this mysterious train ran every night! He wrote to his MP about it and a question was eventually asked in the House of Commons, when it was revealed that the train was confined to services personnel and people on official government business. The southbound train left St Enoch at 9.27 pm called at Kilmarnock and Dumfries and then, from the passengers' point of view, made a non-stop run to Watford Junction. Actually there was a stop abreast of the

27. Up express near Berkhamsted in wintry weather on 6 March 1947, hauled by Jubilee class 3-cylinder 4–6–0 no. 5666, 'Cornwallis'.

LNWR sheds at Carlisle to reman. Thence the non-stop run of 281½ miles from Carlisle no. 12 signal-box to Watford was scheduled in 364 minutes, an average speed of 46.4 mph.

In view of the interest of this service Mr Ivatt arranged for me to have a footplate pass from Glasgow down to Carlisle, and the occasion provided another excellent example of the working of the Stanier Pacific engines. The train was heavy, 463 tons tare, but as the rake included a number of sleeping cars the gross load did not exceed 490 tons. The engine was the last of the original quintet of blue streamliners of 1937, no. 6224 'Princess Alexandra', though by that time painted plain black. Even in the later stages of the war timings over the former Glasgow and South Western line down to

Carlisle had remained nearer to pre-war standards than on almost any other part of the LMS, and because of the very severe Neilston bank, beginning no farther from Glasgow than 6½ miles, and including 3¼ miles as steep as 1 in 67–70, double-heading of heavy trains was frequently necessary. Not so, however, with the Stanier Pacifics even with such a load as 490 tons, in fact when adverse signals brought us practically to a stand at Neilston station, right on the 1 in 70 gradient, the train was lifted away again cleanly and without any slipping when the signal cleared, and we were no more than 3 minutes late leaving Kilmarnock for the south.

The day express from Glasgow St Enoch to St Pancras was then allowed no more than 68 minutes for the 58-mile run to Dumfries, over a road that includes much heavy grading. The 'Ghost Train' was allowed 72 minutes, but had a

28. Down express taking water at Bushey troughs, hauled by Royal Scot class 4–6–0 no. 6123, 'Royal Irish Fusilier'.

stiff initial point-to-point timing of 30 minutes for the first 21.1 miles up to New Cumnock, a section that includes all the hard climbing. The engine was in excellent condition, and expertly driven and fired had no difficulty in passing New Cumnock in 29½ minutes from the start. Thence, down the valley of the Nith, the gradients were favourable to Dumfries, and with 42 minutes allowed for this distance of 36.9 miles there would have been no difficulty in regaining the 3 minutes of arrears with which

we had left Kilmarnock. Indeed, we were approaching Dumfries with about a minute in hand; but the night train to St Pancras, which had left Glasgow only 12 minutes ahead of us and which was, as always, very heavy and crowded, was still in Dumfries station as we approached, and we were held up outside for some minutes awaiting its departure. The net time for the 58-mile run from Kilmarnock was about 66 minutes, because in addition to the traffic delay outside Dumfries we were slackened for track repairs at Carronbridge.

On the final section over which I rode the

49

F. R. Hebron, Rail Archive Stephenson

29. Up Liverpool express passing Tring, hauled by converted Royal Scot 4–6–0 no. 6146, 'The Rifle Brigade'.

delays were frequent. The timetable allowed 48 minutes for the 34.1 miles to the stop at Carlisle no. 12 box where the engine was re-manned. This would have been easy enough with a clear road but we suffered many checks, and were stopped at the entrance to Carlisle passenger station in 47½ minutes. The scheduled time for passing through was 46 minutes. On the downhill sections from New Cumnock the engine was run under easy steam. Speed at no time exceeded 70 mph and for much of the distance the regulator was closed and the engine was coasting. Such gentle working was, however, not possible on the day express to St Pancras, usually worked by the Jubilee class 3-cylinder 4–6–0s, with heavy trains loading to over 400 tons. This was a double-home turn for Leeds men and was often the occasion of very fine work. The initial

30. Southbound Anglo-Scottish express climbing to Shap, hauled by 4–6–2 no. 6233, 'Duchess of Sutherland'.

allowance of 28 minutes for the 21.1 miles up to New Cumnock was something of a counsel of perfection with such loads, and it was usual to drop 2 or 3 minutes; but the track on the ex-G&SW main line – not so heavily worked perhaps on some routes – remained in very good condition, and with some slight bending of the rules on maximum speed such losses could be regained. In fact on one occasion with engine no. 5594, 'Bhopal', hauling 405 tons, when it had taken 32½ minutes to pass New Cumnock,

the ensuing 35.2 miles to Cairn Valley Junction were covered in 30¼ minutes at an average of 70 mph and Dumfries was reached in 65½ minutes from Kilmarnock. Three times on this fast descent of the Nith valley a maximum speed of 80 mph was attained.

The introduction in 1943 of the new taper-boilered Scots together with the two Jubilee class 4–6–0s that were fitted with the same large boiler, with a pressure of 250 lb. per sq. in., was marked by some very fine running on these same trains. On the day express to St Pancras,

51

for example, the rebuilt Jubilee no. 5735 took no assistance up the Neilston bank for a tare load of 366 tons and reached Kilmarnock 4 minutes early. Then from the restart the train passed New Cumnock practically on time in 28¼ minutes, and without exceeding 76 mph afterwards reached Dumfries in 62½ minutes, despite a signal check costing one minute in the final approach. On the longer and far more severe gradients of the Settle and Carlisle line it seemed evident that drivers of the taper-boilered Scots were working them on relatively short cut-offs on the long inclines, and with 400-ton trains the speeds often dropped below 30 mph before the summit points were attained. Furthermore, on the down day express from St Pancras to Glasgow there was an operating problem at times of late running. There was a connecting slow train from Hellifield to Carlisle which, if the express was running more than an hour late from Leeds, had for other reasons to be sent on ahead, with the result that the London–Glasgow express had to stop at all stations between Hellifield and Carlisle for which it was carrying passengers. This usually resulted in a further loss of at least half an hour. It was not often on that train, on which engine and crew worked through to Glasgow, that one got a very good run – taper-boilered Scots or not.

I was fortunate, when arrangements were made for me to ride on the footplate from Leeds to Carlisle, that the departure was only 16 minutes late, and that we had an undelayed run over the mountain section. With engine no. 6117, 'Welsh Guardsman' and a load of 450 tons, speed was allowed to fall to 28 mph on the first long section of 1 in 100 ascent from Settle Junction; but above Horton cut-off was advanced from 22 to 30 per cent, and a fine speed of 36 mph was sustained onwards to Ribblehead. The 46 miles from Hellifield to Appleby, scheduled in 69 minutes, were actually completed in 61½ minutes start to stop. Apart from that one opening out, between Horton and Ribblehead, the engine was worked under relatively easy steam and north of Carlisle, where the load was reduced to 320 tons, the driver used no more than 10 per cent cut-off for long stretches at a time. The engine was then relatively new, and performed easily and economically throughout, bringing the train finally into Glasgow exactly on time. The following table gives an analysis of the engine working over the two sections of the journey.

	Leeds to Carlisle Load 450 tons	Carlisle to Glasgow Load 320 tons
	Miles	Miles
Full gear	1.1	0.3
30% cut-off	5.0	Nil
22% cut-off	11.9	3.9
15% cut-off	30.8	30.7
10% cut-off	38.6	50.9
Steam off, coasting	25.6	29.6
Total	113.0	115.4

6
The Ships in War Service

Until the outbreak of war the LMS owned three Royal Mail packet services between Great Britain and Ireland, and it operated in connection with two more routes via Liverpool – the British and Irish Steam Packet Company, to Dublin, and the Ulster Imperial Line, to Belfast. On the three routes of its own the LMS had ten beautiful ships. There were the three 25-knot mail steamers on the Irish Mail service from Holyhead; the four 'Dukes', *Duke of Argyll*, *Duke of Lancaster*, *Duke of Rothesay* and *Duke of York* on the Heysham–Belfast run, and on the shortest sea passage, between Stranraer and Larne, the *Princess Margaret*, the *Princess Maud* and the *Princess Victoria*. When war came six out of the ten were immediately requisitioned for government service leaving only one each on the Heysham–Belfast, and Stranraer–Larne runs available to the public, and two for the Irish Mail service from Holyhead, which throughout the war remained the most heavily patronised of all the cross-channel routes. The four that remained were the *Cambria* and the *Hibernia*, at Holyhead; the *Duke of Lancaster* at Heysham, and the *Princess Margaret* at Stranraer.

Except for the *Princess Victoria*, which was fitted out as a mine-layer, all the rest were used as troopships, initially for transporting units of the original British Expeditionary Force to France in 1939. The *Princess Victoria* suffered a dose of her own medicine, as it were, striking an enemy mine in the North Sea and sinking with considerable loss of life. The hazards to the remaining five LMS packet steamers came at the time of the Dunkirk evacuation. The *Scotia*, heavily bombed at her moorings, having taken on a large contingent of troops, was so badly damaged that all on board had to be taken off again before the ship itself sank. The *Princess Maud* was also much damaged, though not fatally, and conveyed a large number of men to safety. When, after Dunkirk, an abortive attempt was made to stem the tide of disaster further west in France, that ship and the *Duke of York* were sent to St Valery-en-Caux for another rescue operation, from which they brought home more than 2,000 men, with no worse damage than a few shell holes.

As the pattern of the war at sea changed the importance of the Irish Sea crossing increased, though not for civilian traffic. The Dunkirk evacuation was scarcely completed, and the survivors, who had been brought home in many cases quite regardless of their regimental affiliations, sorted out and regrouped, when urgent preparations had to be made for resisting the expected invasion of this country. When this did

W. Philip Conolly

31. A heavy London express leaving Crewe, hauled by one of the earliest of the Royal Scots to be rebuilt with taper boiler, in a typically dingy state – no. 6120, 'Royal Inniskilling Fusilier'.

not occur, and the military strength of Germany was directed instead against Soviet Russia, the build-up in the United Kingdom continued in readiness for the time when Allied forces would re-enter Europe. It was then that Northern Ireland was brought into extensive use for training troops. Not only was there space there for all the training grounds that were required, but the territory was relatively free from molestation by enemy air attack. It was then that the short sea crossing from Stranraer

to Larne became of vital importance. It was perhaps not by accident that, when in 1938 the LMS had provided Stranraer pier with a ramp and movable gangway over which road vehicles could be driven onto the deck of the steamer alongside, it was made wide and strong enough to carry heavy tanks.

The *Princess Maud*, after her adventures off Dunkirk and St Valery, returned to her own base to assist in the transport of troops and their equipment between Stranraer and Larne; but the importance and volume of the developing traffic was signalised by the transfer, from the English

54

32. The launch on the Clyde in 1928 of the only one of the LMS ships to remain on the Heysham–Belfast run during the war – the turbine steamer *Duke of Argyll*.

Channel, of two ships originally on the Dover–Dunkirk train ferry service of the Southern – the *Shepperton Ferry* and the *Twickenham Ferry*. At Stranraer there was, of course, no question of transhipping rolling stock, because the difference in the rail gauges in Britain and Ireland alone would make this impracticable; but they were well adapted for carrying tanks. These ships were later fitted with travelling cranes, running on tracks extending the entire length of the vessel and jutting out beyond the stern. This made possible the embarking and disembarking of heavy rolling stock that could be lifted from, and placed upon, tracks adjacent to the steamer berths.

Quite apart from ships, the vital position that Stranraer was assuming in cross-channel traffic, often of whole divisions at a time, may well cause railway enthusiasts with a knowledge of how things were managed before the war to wonder how on earth the *railway* traffic was handled over the lengthy single-tracked

33. The Heysham–Belfast steamer *Duke of York* in peacetime. During the war she assisted in the evacuation from Dunkirk, and afterwards at St Valery-en-Caux.

approaches, southward from Girvan and westward from Dumfries, converging at Challoch Junction, onto the final single-tracked bottleneck of 7 miles from there into Stranraer. In prewar years the lines in question were sparsely used, but very careful planning was nevertheless essential in pathing the numerous specials to avoid congestion. Some improvements in the signalling arrangements were made at Challoch Junction, but in readiness for the arrival of the Americans an entirely new port facility was created at Cairnryan, on the eastern shore of Loch Ryan, and on the seaward side of Stranraer itself. It is a reminder of the vital importance of the Stranraer–Larne sea route that

the very first American soldiers to arrive in the United Kingdom, as early as 26 January 1942 after the Pearl Harbour incident, disembarked at Belfast. Later in the war when the build-up towards the D-day landings of 1944 was progressing, the government requisitioned the last LMS passenger ship to remain in civilian service at Stranraer, the *Princess Margaret*, and sent as substitute a Thames pleasure steamer, the *Royal Daffodil*.

The great estuary and magnificently sheltered anchorage of the Firth of Clyde provided an ideal arrival point for the largest liners acting as troopships. The famous Cunard White Star 'Queens', painted battleship-grey, brought the Americans over a whole division at a time in each ship. But there was no berth that they

34. The Irish Mail steamer *Scotia* at Holyhead in peacetime. She was bombed and sunk at her moorings during the Dunkirk evacuation.

could get alongside and they had to anchor in the inner basin, opposite Greenock, and discharge their cargoes, human or otherwise, into tenders that plied between the big ships and the piers at Gourock, Greenock (Princes Pier), and outside LMS territory on the right bank of the firth at Craigendoran and Kilcreggan. The Ministry of Transport set up an organisation known as the Clyde Anchorage Emergency Port. It was intended to deal with the unloading of large vessels that could not reach a quay. Gourock, perhaps the best equipped of the passenger packet stations, was greatly expanded. Although the big ships could not berth alongside, provision was made for many more small ships than previously to disembark troops simultaneously. Princes Pier was a well-equipped steamer port but the railway approach to it, over the heavily graded line of the former Glasgow and South Western Railway, made it less convenient than Gourock for the rapid dispatch of heavy troop trains. Many of the railway steamers previously operating on the Clyde were requisitioned and went south, and the *Juno*, of the former G&SW fleet, was bombed and sunk at her moorings in the Thames.

35. The *Princess Maud*, in peacetime on the Stranraer–Larne run. Though heavily damaged at Dunkirk she was able to evacuate a large number of troops, and afterwards went to St Valery to join the *Duke of York*, whence she brought home 2,000 men.

Although it could in no way be claimed that the *Queen Elizabeth* was an LMS ship she became so closely associated through her voyages from the Clyde to and from the USA, and the men she brought over for onward conveyance by the LMS, as to be almost an adopted child. On the outbreak of war she was still uncom-

pleted at the Clydebank yard of John Brown Ltd. While she remained there she presented a sitting, and very prominent, target for air attack; but fortunately she was completed and steamed away to New York before the severe air raids on Clydeside that came in March 1941. The date of her departure was a well-kept secret, even to the extent of allowing an unreliable rumour to spread which drew hundreds to vantage points along the river to watch

36. Stranraer pier, with war supplies being loaded on to one of the former Southern Railway train ferry ships temporarily transferred from Dover.

for the ship that did not come. In his auto-biography, *A lifetime with Locomotives*, the late R. C. Bond tells how a reliable tip a few days later made a visit to Bowling signal-box very worthwhile, and what an astonishing sight it was to see the great grey-painted ship pass on her way to the sea.

In the second volume of this work I referred to the improvements made at Fleetwood docks for dealing with the fish traffic and the fuelling of the trawler fleet. Recalling the great work done by the fishing fleets of the East Coast ports in minesweeping during the First World War a high proportion of the fleets at Hull and Grimsby had been requisitioned in 1939 for similar duties. Equally because of the greater safety in operation a number of trawlers were transferred to Fleetwood, and activities there tremendously increased. In the four years before the outbreak of war the landings had averaged 66,000 tons, but by 1943 this had been stepped up to no less than 136,000 tons. While this did not approach the pre-war landings at the major fishing ports of Hull and Grimsby, it was more than double the landings at those ports in the restricted and difficult conditions of wartime. The investment in new facilities at Fleetwood made by the LMS in the 1930s paid off hand-somely in the wartime emergency.

7
Brickbats and Bouquets

One of the things we were supposed to be fighting for was for freedom – freedom of action (within the law!), freedom of speech; so that no one could really mind at a little heartfelt grumbling as the war progressed, privately or otherwise. And it is no more than natural that the railways of this country, always good for a knock, came in for a share of such criticism. It was not to be expected that the man constrained to nothing more comfortable than a stand in the corridor would be able to appreciate the finer points of railway operation in wartime, nor of the colossal difficulties under which it was being conducted; and one could have some sympathy with the man who wrote a letter to his favourite newspaper complaining of this and that. Nevertheless, one would expect newspaper editors, who after all have a responsibility to their readers to present a reasonably fair picture, especially at a time when national unity was so essential, to inquire a little into accounts of exceptional experience on the part of correspondents before splashing them into the prominence of a spiteful leading article.

Today, forty years later, it is incredible to recall that on 17 November 1940, when troop movements and transport of war-freight were extremely heavy and difficult, and when the night blitz was in full blast, a Sunday paper of wide circulation, whose shame I will spare by letting it remain anonymous, published a leading article entitled, 'A Story of a Railway Journey', of which the following extracts will give some idea of the seething indignation it created on the LMS.

Here is the simple story of a main line express train which made the journey from a provincial city to London a day or two ago . . . The train pulled out of the station at 9.45 am. It was due in London at 1.50 pm. At one point on the journey that train stood still for more than an hour. Then it went backwards for several miles. It eventually reached London at 8.0 pm – six hours late on a journey scheduled to last four hours. The train was packed. At many stations it stopped to pick up still more passengers. Although the news could have been telephoned all down the line that passengers, women and children, were already herded like cattle in the corridors, no attempt was made to fix additional coaches to the train . . . There was a restaurant car on the train. Those who were rich enough to pay for the meal could get lunch in it. But after lunch the restaurant car went out of business . . . When the train at last reached London most of the passengers had spent 10 hours in it without food or drink of any kind . . . The train arrived in Town when the night raid was in

H. C. Casserley

37. Ex-Highland Railway 4–4–0 no. 14391, 'Loch Shin', withdrawn for scrapping in 1941, but reinstated in 1942, and repaired for further service at the Bow Works of the former North London Railway.

full blast. No arrangements of any sort had been made to convey the passengers to their several destinations . . . This kind of resolute and calculated indifference to the comfort or convenience of their customers prevails over the whole of the British Railways. It exists on the branch lines and suburban lines as well as on the main roads of railway traffic . . . Goods traffic is in chaotic condition . . . The railways must realise that the public expects them now not only to maintain a peace-time efficiency, but to improve upon it . . . Let this also be

said, the railways not only let down the nation by their present parrot-cry of 'Don't you know there is a war on?' as an excuse for 10,000 instances of avoidable inefficiency, but also lose the goodwill of the public . . . The busmen who drive their vehicles to schedule through the bombardment, the firemen, the factory and munition workers, are all laying up for themselves an immense store of public sympathy by the way they carry on their duties . . . Only the railwaymen . . . are in disgrace. They may come to be regarded as people who, having failed the nation in its danger hour, have no claims upon the nation's bounty when the danger is past.

38. Southbound freight train near Berkhamsted hauled by
ex-LNW 0–8–0 no. 9127.

Now, believe it or not, this journey was that of
the 9.45 am from Manchester to Euston, via
Stoke, on the very morning after the terrible air
raid on Coventry, in which the damage to the
railway lines in the neighbourhood, as described
in chapter 3 of this book, was quite exceptional
in its intensity. In view of the vast number of
incidents with which railwaymen in the area had
to deal it would have been quite understandable
if two *unexploded* bombs on the main line
between Nuneaton and Rugby had not been
located by day break; but this was not so, and
before leaving Manchester, on time, a rerouteing
was planned, diverting the train from Nuneaton
to Wigston, and thence via the Midland Counties
line to Rugby. The increased mileage was about
twenty, and the journey time expected to be
increased by one hour. Of course, all other

traffic over the Trent Valley line would have to
be similarly diverted.

After leaving Stoke only a few minutes late,
and with no standing passengers, the train was
stopped by signal at Stone to be informed that
two more unexploded bombs had been found
near the Nuneaton–Wigston line, near enough
for the bomb disposal experts to forbid any rail
traffic. It was a situation from which immediate
improvisation was impossible. But after a delay
that was by no means inordinate in the circumstances the train was drawn back to Stoke, and
then taken down the North Staffordshire line,
through Uttoxeter to Burton-on-Trent, and
thence over the Midland line via Ashby de la
Zouch and Coalville to Leicester. After this very
unusual route it was a relatively simple matter to
get the train back to the North Western main
line at Rugby, though for every section it would

39. Up Midland line express, Nottingham–St Pancras
near Edwalton, hauled by Class 5 4–6–0 no. 4818.

T. G. Hepburn, Rail Archive Stephenson

have been necessary to provide for road pilot-
men at very short notice, and as previously
emphasised, not for this train only! At stop-
ping stations, made for locomotive manning
purposes, the train would naturally be boarded
by waiting passengers, while the final hazard
was in the approach to London after dark and
under red alert conditions, involving then a
maximum speed of only 15 mph. As to the

unspeakable comparison between railway and
bus services, of which one had nothing but the
highest admiration for the latter, I wonder
how many buses were running to schedule in
Coventry on that gruesome morning!

I have pilloried this particular case of blatant
journalistic ignorance and anti-railway prejudice, because it was typical of an attitude that
became more pronounced as the war began to
near its victorious end and political pressures

40. Yarmouth–Nottingham train near Widmerpool, hauled
by 4F 0–6–0 no. 4412.

T. G. Hepburn, Rail Archive Stephenson

41. A heavy northbound freight train climbing Shap, hauled by Patriot class 4–6–0 no. 5542 and banked in rear.

W. Philip Conolly

began to arise. Against this I shall never forget the outstanding BBC feature broadcast 'Junction X', which Desmond Shawe-Taylor, radio critic of the *Sunday Times*, described as

. . . a beautiful piece of radio with the grasp and emotional power of a good film documentary. I wish I had more space to dwell on the facilities of this picture of British railways under the stress of war; the complicated interlocking organisation, the superficial 'flap', the fundamental calm. Little as I know about railways, 'Junction X' rings true; furthermore, it is grand entertainment and first-rate propaganda for the man on the platform. Such a feature deserves not one, but half a dozen repetitions.

'Junction X', written and produced by Cecil McGivern, described modestly as 'a dramatisation of events that occurred at a vital crossroads on the path to victory on a certain day in 1944 between the hours of 10 a.m. and 10 p.m.', was based on activities at Crewe not long before D-day.

The next occasion to which I must refer might have called forth brickbats from some of the passengers concerned, but which brought almost fulsome praise from a knowledgeable traveller who wrote of the experience to the journal of the Stephenson Locomotive Society. It concerned the 1 pm Glasgow express from Euston at the end of August 1942, which on that day was loaded to seventeen vehicles, 510 tons tare, and with the usual crowding probably not less than 550 tons full. The engine was a

65

42. At Bushey troughs. A train of coal empties, surprisingly on the down *fast* line, hauled by ex-LNW 0–8–0 no. 9060 and an 8F Stanier 2–8–0 no. 8136.

F. R. Hebron, Rail Archive Stephenson

Royal Scot, no. 6144, and began well, passing Bletchley 5 minutes early on this wartime schedule. Then delays supervened and when at 2.43 pm, 103 minutes from Euston, the train was stopped by signal outside Rugby it was evident something was amiss with the engine. It had to be detached. In North Western days Rugby was a major locomotive centre and many important trains changed engines there; but with the introduction of long through workings in the 1930s the representatives of the largest express passenger classes were transferred else-

where. In any case it would have been unlikely in wartime for there to have been any spare engines on hand.

In the 1930s the north end standing pilot was usually a Midland Compound, but on this occasion nothing larger than an old Midland 7-foot Class 2 4–4–0 was available, no. 524, and to this the driver and fireman of the Scot transferred. A gallant effort was made with this seventeen-coach train, but it was inevitable that a good deal of time would be lost. On the down gradients of the Trent Valley speeds of 53 to 54 mph were attained, and Rugeley, 41¾ miles, was passed in 57 minutes from the start; but bad signal checks at Stafford and Great Bridgeford made a crippling prelude to the ascent to Whitmore. Although it sounded as though the engine was being driven absolutely all out the speed did not average more than 37 mph from Norton Bridge to the summit. But the driver and fireman never gave up trying, and on the descent to Crewe they attained 61 mph. The total time for the 75.5 miles from Rugby was 113 minutes, but the checks around Stafford cost at least 6 minutes, leaving a net average speed of 42 mph. Seeing that the engine was hauling at least *double* what one would normally expect for a 2P it was a highly commendable effort. The correspondent who recorded it concluded, 'A missed connection was nothing to pay for such a thrill'. Though it is doubtful if many of the passengers would have shared his enthusiasm for an arrival just one hour late.

In the July 1941 issue of the Journal of the Stephenson Locomotive Society I myself wrote:

In the most favourable circumstances, cross-country services are not the easiest on which to maintain punctual running, and it was in some trepidation that I went on a journey of this kind in recent months, especially considering that one district *en route* had been heavily engaged with the Luftwaffe only two days before I travelled. Both outward and

return journeys were, however, a pleasant surprise; for not only was the locomotive work interesting, and at times most enterprising, but we kept remarkably good time.

Bound for Chesterfield, and travelling by the 3.5 pm express from Bristol we had a load of 360 tons hauled by 5X engine no. 5627, 'Sierra Leone'. There were many checks, in a journey that included stops at Mangotsfield, Gloucester, Cheltenham, Ashchurch, Bromsgrove, Birmingham, Tamworth, Burton, and Derby. These totalled up to a loss of about 25 minutes in running; but with the enterprising locomotive work we were only 5 minutes late on arrival at Chesterfield. From Birmingham to Derby we had the help of a 'Black Five' 4–6–0, double-heading our 5X, to avoid light working on an unbalanced duty. The return journey, with an absolutely packed train of 420 tons, and engine no. 5724, 'Warspite', was equally good. At Birmingham another coach was added, bringing the load up to 450 tons and a second 5X was coupled on ahead. The power thenceforward available was used to good effect in recovering the time lost by signal and permanent way checks. Although not very inspiring by pre-war standards it was good in the circumstances prevailing during the early months of 1941 to reach one's destination so nearly to time, in both directions.

8
A Time of Transition

The end of the war in Europe brought no respite to the railways of Britain – least of all, perhaps, to the LMS. Although the black-out was ended, there was no longer danger from flying bombs and V2 rockets and no reports of casualties in the armies advancing towards the Rhine, the conditions under which the home railways were operating were in many ways more difficult than ever. During the war everyone was pulling together. Most of the grumbling was good natured, but once the wartime tension was relaxed, every kind of animosity seemed to be let loose. The unheeding public, heartily backed up and nourished by a hostile press, seemed to expect pre-war standards to be restored at once, while for the railway managements the result of the British General Election of 1945, by making early nationalisation a certainty, clouded the entire prospect of post-war reconstruction. Further-more, the shock to international opinion, con-sequent upon Churchill's 'dismissal', and the ending of American aid, imposed upon this country a situation of deep austerity; and although the more cheerful amongst us could laugh at the substitution for the wartime slogan, 'Britain can take it' by the post-war 'Britain can lump it', it was all rather depressing.

The extent to which the physical resources of the LMS had been strained was shown in the number of temporary speed restrictions on the West Coast Main Line. When in the autumn of 1945 a Parliamentary question was put to the new Minister of Transport (who of course had not a clue about the running of railways!) as to why the 10 am express from Glasgow to Euston was continuously late, all he could do was to promise to make inquiries. Any regular traveller who took no more than the most perfunctory interest in train running could have told him readily enough! But the war had taken its toll upon human beings as much as on fixed equip-ment and rolling stock, and on 12 October 1945, at the relatively early age of fifty-eight, Mr C. E. Fairburn, the Chief Mechanical and Electrical Engineer of the company died. His death, so soon after the war, recalls the death of C. J. Bowen Cooke of the LNWR soon after the end of the First World War, both events robbing the railway world of outstanding personalities at a time when momentous changes were not far ahead.

Fairburn's unexpected and untimely death caused some distinct heart-searching among the higher echelons of the LMS over the appoint-ment of a successor. Sir Harold Hartley, who had been primarily responsible for securing the services of Mr Fairburn in 1934, was known to

43. C. E. Fairburn, Chief Mechanical Engineer 1944–5.

be not in favour of a return to a more conventional type of railway chief mechanical engineer, whereas the two immediate candidates were H. G. Ivatt, and, of course, R. A. Riddles, who had returned to the LMS from the Ministry of Supply in 1943 to become Chief Stores Superintendent. Opinion at the top levels of LMS management went against Sir Harold Hartley, and he resigned as Vice-President to join the board of British Overseas Airways Corporation, and. there was con-

siderable speculation in railway circles as to who would get the job of CME, particularly as no appointment was made for some little time after Fairburn's death. Late in January 1946 it was announced that Ivatt had been appointed Chief Mechanical Engineer, and R. C. Bond went from Crewe to be Mechanical Engineer (Locomotive Works). He was later appointed deputy Chief Mechanical Engineer. A pleasing inclusion in the New Year's Honours List of 1946, and a flashback to earlier days in the CME's department of the LMS was the conferment of the CBE on Major H. P. M. Beames who succeeded Bowen Cooke as CME of the LNWR in 1920, and who was deputy CME of the LMS from 1931 to 1934. In his retirement, during the war, he was Chairman of the Emergency Committee of the County of Cheshire.

The resignation of Sir Harold Hartley from the Executive Committee left that body with only two Vice-Presidents, T. W. Royle and G. L. Darbyshire, the last mentioned gentleman having succeeded Sir Ernest Lemon on the Executive in 1943. At the end of April 1946 two additional Vice-Presidents were appointed, bringing the Executive up to its normal full strength; these were F. A. Pope and R. A. Riddles, both life-long railwaymen and both originating on the London and North Western. Pope had a very full and varied career rising to Superintendent of Operation (LMS) from 1938–40. In 1940 he was Director of Railways with the British Expeditionary Force and then Manager of the NCC section of the LMS in Northern Ireland. Before the war he served for five years on the Nigerian Railways and twice visited India, and he went there again in 1944 to become Regional Port Director, Calcutta. The career of R. A. Riddles as a distinguished locomotive engineer is well known, and in 1946 his greatest work was yet to come, after nationalisation.

The summer and autumn of 1945 had been

marred by two bad accidents to Anglo-Scottish expresses. Both were caused by running through signals and in both cases the underlying reason for this remained unexplained through the deaths of the enginemen concerned. The first occurred on 21 July with the 1 pm express from Glasgow to Euston, at Ecclefechan, the first station south of Lockerbie, when the train travelling at 60 to 65 mph passed the distant signal at caution, overran the home signals and collided at full speed with a freight train, which was setting back into the up siding to clear the road for the express to pass. The express engine, non-streamlined 4–6–2 no. 6231, 'Duchess of Atholl', came to rest on its right hand side, 138 yards ahead of the point of collision, badly damaged and both enginemen were killed. It was probably the distance the engine travelled after striking the freight train, and driving its engine forward more than 100 yards that saved the express from serious damage, and although thirty-one passengers were injured all had left hospital within ten days.

The Inspecting Officer of the Ministry of Transport devoted much attention to the sighting of the three signals that were disregarded, namely the Ecclefechan up distant and the outer and inner home signals, but concluded they were adequate, and that the distant was sufficiently in rear of the outer home to provide adequate braking distance at a speed of 60 to 65 mph. Several witnesses, however, referred to a pall of black smoke enveloping the engine as it approached; but no significance seems to have been attached to what, in my own opinion, would have been a very vital piece of evidence. A few months after this accident I had occasion to ride on the footplate of one of these engines, no. 6251, from Carlisle to Glasgow, on a wet night, when the exhaust steam was beating down and obscuring the look-out ahead to such an extent that the driver had frequently to shut

44. H. G. Ivatt, Chief Mechanical Engineer 1946–8.

off steam to get a sight of the signals. This, as was also the case with the engine involved at Ecclefechan, was before these engines were fitted with smoke-deflecting screens beside the smokebox. The Ecclefechan accident also occurred on a wet day, when there would have been much exhaust steam from the locomotive condensing around the boiler. After my own experience on the footplate of no. 6251 I wrote personally to Ivatt expressing my apprehension, and I was very glad to learn later that they had decided to put smoke-deflecting plates on.

45. Smoke troubles on the Duchesses: how the exhaust clung to the boiler top before smoke deflectors were added.

Then soon after dawn on Sunday 30 September there was a far worse accident from a driver apparently disregarding signals. It can be classed with those notorious derailments of the pre-Grouping era, at Grantham, Salisbury and Shrewsbury, when drivers had run inexplicably hard in the most unsuitable places and wrecked their trains with grievous loss of life. All of them were inexplicable because neither the driver nor the fireman survived. It was the same at Bourne End. This was a signal-box intermediate between Berkhamsted and Hemel Hempstead controlling crossover junctions between the fast and the slow lines; and on that particular Sunday morning all up expresses were being crossed onto the slow line because of engineering occupation ahead. Speed over the crossovers was limited to 25 mph but the evidence was that the up Perth sleeping car express, hauled by Royal Scot class 4–6–0 no. 6157 took the crossover at

46. One of the later Duchess class 4–6–2s no. 6252,
'City of Leicester', built at Crewe in 1944.

60 mph at least. The engine survived the first sharp turn-out to the left but then, being in a very unstable condition, overturned to the left at the right hand trailing junction. Unfortunately the line is on a shallow embankment at this point, and the engine fell down the bank dragging part of the train to its destruction in the field below. No fewer than thirty-eight persons were killed.

No explanation was afterwards forthcoming as to why an experienced driver with an impeccable record should have run as he did. The morning was fine, and the enginemen of two preceding trains which had been similarly diverted said they had no difficulty in sighting the signals that had warned them of the divergence. In any case the movement had been advised in the weekly notice issued to all drivers over the route, and the driver of the Perth express should have been aware of it. While the signalling on that section was then manual block, generally with semaphore signals, the lead-up to the actual splitting signals at the junction was by means of four-aspect colour-lights; and these were all correctly displayed on the morning in question. The Inspecting Officer of the Ministry of Transport in reporting upon the accident expressed himself as quite satisfied

47. The serious accident at Bourne End crossing, near Hemel Hempstead, on Sunday 30 September 1945. The derailed engine, 4–6–0 no. 6157 'The Royal Artilleryman', almost buried under the wreckage.

with the layout of the signals and their visibility, and suggested that this was an occasion when automatic train control giving audible warnings in the cab as on the Great Western Railway would have been invaluable. While some incident in the locomotive cab might have temporarily diverted the attention of the engine-

men, the audible warning would have alerted them to the imminent danger.

Although it was not until the terrible double collision at Harrow, in 1952, that the need for automatic train control reached crisis point, there was a certain amount of criticism of the LMS for not having pressed ahead with its development, following the installation of the inductive system on the Southend line before the war. It was, of course, no more than natural

73

48. One of the latest examples of Class 4 2–6–4 tank class, no. 2227, built in 1946 at Derby, with self-cleaning plates in the smokebox.

T. G. Hepburn, Rail Archive Stephenson

that outsiders wondered why the Great Western system had not been adopted, when so many other Great Western ideas had been brought to the LMS by Stanier. But while the principle had been accepted there was deep-rooted opposition to the idea of a contact ramp for the link up between engine and signals. While some of this came from prejudice and from the parochialism between the old railways that was eventually only broken down by nationalisation, in the long term, and with the advantage of hindsight, the LMS were right to oppose the contact ramp

in view of the difficulties that would have arisen with electrification, and the undesirability of having a contact system when speeds advanced to the region of 125 mph or more.

So far as the development of automatic train control was concerned, while it is understandable that this work had to be suspended during the war, it was taken up again in 1944 and discussed with potential contractors. It was, however, one of those projects that was slowed down at the time of nationalisation, when in the light of future standardisation very serious account had to be taken of the existence of the Great Western system installed throughout the entire main line network of that company.

9
Prospects of Nationalisation

As nationalisation loomed ahead the LMS, administratively, was strong in most fields. In mechanical and electrical engineering Ivatt's new team was united, purposeful and forward looking; and if, to outward appearances, the same could not be said of civil engineering few outside the railway service realised the terrific beating the track had taken during the war, from the sheer volume of traffic, and from the extent to which maintenance had to be deferred. This is not to suggest that any part of the line had been allowed to deteriorate into a dangerous condition. Careful invigilating had shown clearly enough where speed restrictions had to be imposed. It was just that the men and materials were not available to do the necessary repairs. And then on top of the wartime arrears came the fearful winter of 1946/7, with prolonged frost and snow seriously affecting the track formation in many areas.

It was in signalling that the LMS seemed to be lagging behind. This was all the more surprising in view of the record of A. F. Bound before his appointment as Chief Signal and Telegraph Engineer, and of his subsequent appointment as a Chief Officer of the Company. After the introduction of speed-signalling aspects at Mirfield, as related in volume 2 of this work, his subsequent activities seemed pedestrian by comparison with what his contemporaries on other British railways were doing. As always he remained a frequent speaker at meetings where signalling was discussed; but, whether from deeply felt disapproval or pure 'sour-grapes', he became strongly critical of some of his fellow signal engineers. Indeed of one meeting, at the Institution of Civil Engineers of all places, an eminent engineer with whom I was closely associated said that at one stage the proceedings degenerated to the level of a village debating society! In 1943 Bound had retired and was succeeded by his deputy, W. Wood, who did little more than hold the fort until nationalisation.

To some extent signalling on the LMS was influenced by the system of traffic control that had been standardised. This was a development of the Midland Railway system dating back to the days of Sir Cecil Paget as Chief General Superintendent. In its equipment and general operating technique it differed from that in use on two out of the three areas of the LNER – North Eastern and Scottish – in which the

49. One of the two Jubilee class 3-cylinder 4–6–0s to be fitted with the large taper boiler later used on the converted Royal Scot class, no. 5736, 'Phoenix', here seen in the post-war livery of lined black.

H. C. Casserley Collection

graphical system of train movement recording was used. On the LMS the minute-to-minute movement of trains was registered by moving tags along lines on control boards representing the track configurations. The operating philosophy was to use a multiplicity of smaller signal-boxes at large areas of concentration, rather than one huge central box, as on the LNER at York.

A welcome return to pre-war operating conditions in 1946 was the restoration of the travelling post office services, including the famous West Coast 'Special', carrying nought but postal traffic between Euston and Perth.

This train, in the down direction, had some sharp timings north of Preston, with an allowance of 101 minutes over the 90.1 miles to Carlisle, and 88 minutes for the continuation, over Beattock summit to Carstairs (73.2 miles). Both these timings were considerably faster than those of any passenger trains at that time. Furthermore, from Perth northwards, where the train carried a passenger section, only 95 minutes were allowed for the 89.8 miles to Aberdeen. This required locomotive performance fully up to the fastest needed over that route in pre-war years. The down and up 'Special' TPO trains were not the only ones to which TPO carriages were restored. Of the others one of the most important was the 'Midland TPO', operating between Bristol and

50. The new District Control Office, Stoke-on-Trent.

Newcastle, while feeder services to the 'Special', originated at Cardiff, Aberystwyth, Bangor, Birmingham and Lincoln.

Very soon after the war a scheme of steam locomotive standardisation was worked out, which, with one exception, could have provided all the immediate requirements of British Railways after nationalisation. Seven of the ten types proposed were existing standards from the Stanier regime; in fact the only Stanier design that it was not proposed to continue was the Jubilee 3-cylinder 4–6–0, though it was intended to reboiler all the Baby Scots, with the large 250-lb. taper boilers used on the Royal

Scot replacements. The seven existing types were the Duchess class 4–6–2, the taper-boilered Scot, the 'Black Five' 4–6–0, the 8F 2–8–0, the Class 4 2–6–4 tank, the Class 3 0–6–0 tank (Jinty) and the Class 2 outside cylinder 'dock' shunting 0–6–0 tank. The new designs were the small Class 2 2–6–0 and 2–6–2 tanks introduced by Ivatt, for light branch and secondary services, and a new design of 2–6–0, of Class 4 capacity, which did not appear until the time of nationalisation. It was interesting to see that the Class 5 2–6–0s of the Horwich and early Stanier types were no longer considered a standard. In its proposals for locomotive

51. The post-war 'Royal Scot' at Bushey, hauled by ·
de-streamlined 4–6–2 no. 6245, 'City of London' in lined
black livery.

standardisation the LMS had no maximum power mixed traffic design, an equivalent of the Gresley V2 2–6–2 of the LNER.

The small Class 2 engines, which appeared first at the end of 1946, were intended as a modern replacement for the many older designs of pre-Grouping vintage that were becoming obsolescent, and the new 2–6–0 was suitable for use on practically all parts of the system, having a maximum axle load of no more than 12 tons. With cylinders 16 in. diameter by 24 in. stroke, 5 ft diameter coupled wheels and a combined heating surface of 1159.5 sq. ft it was a tiny little thing by contemporary standards. I made some footplate runs with them on the Penrith–Keswick line, and found that the ex-LNWR 18-inch 0–6–0s ('Cauliflowers') could do equally well on the heavy gradients of that route. But some real shocks were in store for the LMS when, just after nationalisation, it was proposed to draft engines of this class into Western Region branch line service in South Wales, and it was found that they could not undertake duties which the ex-GWR Dean goods 0–6–0s were performing with ease. It is, however, taking the story beyond that of strictly LMS history to add that one of these engines was submitted to analytical examination on the Swindon testing plant, and its steaming capacity greatly improved in consequence.

The 2–6–2 tank was identical to the 2–6–0 in all its main proportions, except that the presence of the side-tanks increased the maximum axle loads to 13¼ tons. Both the 2–6–0 and the 2–6–2 tank were fitted with rocker grates and self-emptying ashpans, and generally in keeping with the forward looking locomotive policy of the LMS. They were neat and compact in appearance and very comfortable engines to ride. The 2–6–0 had an entirely new design of tender, to provide a good look-out and comfort for the men when running tender first. This was a much appreciated feature on a line like that between Penrith and Keswick, where the conditions of working naturally came to be compared with those on the old North Western

'Cauliflowers'. But for sheer guts in handling a load there was little to choose between old and new.

In 1946 details were made public of two important track widening schemes carried out during the war, but hitherto not disclosed for security reasons. These were the quadrupling of the line between Gloucester and Cheltenham, which was used by both Great Western and LMS traffic, and the widening of the short but extremely serious double-line bottleneck between the Port Carlisle and Etterby Junctions, north of Carlisle. No more than a glance at the map of the first-named instance is needed to emphasise what an extremely awkward and hampering stretch the Gloucester–Cheltenham section could be under heavy wartime utilisation. Indeed, the map does not tell the whole story because the line marked 'To Ledbury' is actually the old South Wales main line of the GWR, while the line through Cheltenham South is the old M&SW Joint, upgraded as a wartime route to the south coast ports. It can well be imagined how traffic from so many points could impinge upon that double-line bottleneck. Although the widening was a joint

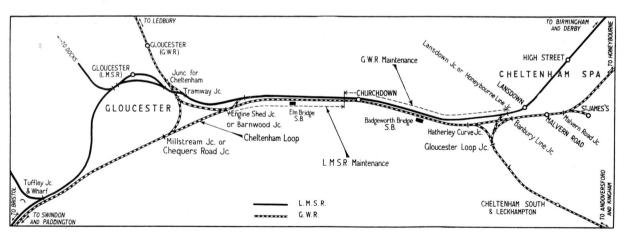

Layout of GWR and LMSR lines between Gloucester and Cheltenham after quadrupling.

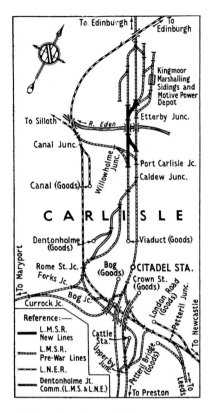

Railways in and around Carlisle.

task was the crossing of the River Eden about 150 feet wide and close to the steep Scaur on its right bank. Through this eminence the railway is carried in a deep cutting. The new bridge was built on a curve of 42 chains radius, with the object of keeping it as far as possible from the old one. This was an ARP measure to reduce the risk that the same bomb might damage both bridges; but it proved a boon during construction because cranes could operate on the new bridge without fouling the main line.

Quite apart from the type of labour that was available the constructional work proved more difficult than was anticipated. It was at first intended that the new bridge should be carried entirely on concrete piles; but the surface of the rock, a marlstone of great age, was found to be so close to the bed of the river on the north side, adjacent to the Scaur, that piles could be used only on the southern half, where they could be driven through the alluvium and gravel and a short depth into the softened upper layers of the rock. The four northern piers were constructed with mass concrete foundations on the marl, within steel-piled cofferdams for the three that were actually in the river. While the bridge over the river provided the major problems, the map shows how its completion enabled greatly improved track connections to be laid in and the bottleneck eliminated. The reference on the map to Kingmoor marshalling sidings refers, of course, to the old yard beside the one-time Caledonian engine sheds. The modern mechanised yard is on the west side of the main line north of the overbridge that carried the LNER line to Edinburgh.

The winter timetables introduced in October 1946 showed some welcome improvements over those of 1945, though overall times between London and the principal cities on the system were still very much slower than the best services of 1938–9. In weekly train mileage,

project of the two companies the work was designed and supervised by the Chief Civil Engineer of the LMS, and included some important track remodelling at Hatherly Junction, to provide for the minimum of surface connections between the Great Western and LMS streams of traffic.

At Carlisle, where the situation can be studied from the accompanying map, it might have seemed a relatively simple job. So it could have been in normal conditions; but in 1942–3 the scarcity of labour was acute, and a large part of the work was done by casual labour – the last scrapings of the labour market. It can readily be appreciated that they sorely taxed the humour and patience of the supervisory staff. The main

80

52. One of Class 5 mixed traffic 4–6–0s, no. 4758, fitted with roller bearing axles throughout.

amounting to 1,544,000 miles, the total had risen to 88 per cent of that run before the war during the winter months, but the speeds were very much less. The down 'Royal Scot', for example, took 8½ hours from Euston to Glasgow, while the corresponding up train benefiting from its long non-stop run from Carlisle to London took only 8¼ hours. There was considerable improvement by the Midland route to Scotland, with the 9.55 am from St Pancras reaching Glasgow St Enoch at 7.23 pm, just 79 minutes acceleration. The speed of the up night express from St Enoch was not exactly heroic, taking 10 hours 5 minutes to St Pancras, but it did nevertheless represent an acceleration of 95 minutes on the previous time! The best times of 8¼ to 8½ hours to Glasgow, 3¾ to 4 hours to Liverpool and Manchester, and 2 hours 10 minutes from Euston to Birmingham indicate the general standards of service offered in the winter of 1946/7 on the

81

National Railway Museum

53. One of the last two Duchess class 4–6–2 locomotives, no. 6256, 'Sir William A. Stanier F.R.S.', built at Crewe with roller bearing axles, and self-cleaning plates in the smokebox.

West Coast route. By the Midland 3 hours 18 minutes to Sheffield and 4 hours 13 minutes to Leeds were the best times.

It will no doubt come as a surprise to present day readers to learn that even in the autumn of 1946 the LMS, like the other railways, was still carrying a substantial volume of traffic for the Forces. In giving evidence before the Railway Charges Consultative Committee in September 1946, in respect of proposals for adjustments in railway fares and charges Mr F. A. Pope, a Vice-President of the Company, stated that they were then running, on an average, 550 special troop trains a *week*, while special freight trains for the Forces still amounted to some 300 trains a week. It was not only on the rails that LMS equipment was still required for military services. The steamship services to Northern Ireland were still severely restricted by the retention of several of the largest LMS steamers in government service.

54. One of the Ivatt Class 2 2–6–0s no. 6416 on trial on
the Great Central line, early in 1948, leaving Nottingham
Victoria for Mansfield.

10
A Last Appraisal

The year 1947 opened amid a welter of Parliamentary slanging matches before the Transport Bill received its second reading in the House of Commons. Even in retrospect, thirty-three years later, the affair makes depressing reading, and it is sad to recall that an industry that served the country so magnificently during the greatest emergency it had ever faced should have been so besmirched with political mud-slinging in order to reduce to the barest minimum the compensation to be paid to the proprietors for the taking over of their property. In recalling the LMS, like the other great railways of Britain, the public naturally thinks of its hardware and the services it rendered to passengers and traders; we remember the uniformed staff at the stations, the train crews, and the more senior grades – names only to many railway enthusiasts, but familiar enough through the railway press. Little thought, however, was given to the *owners*, the men and women whose money was invested in the railways, and who, even in the best of times, derived very little from their investment. It was these who got such a raw deal when the Transport Bill eventually received the Royal Assent on 6 August 1947.

In personnel at all levels, and in its equipment, the LMS made a massive contribution to the nationalised British railway system as it came into being in January 1948, and in its last year of independence there were some interesting moments. In early February there came a spell of weather that in many areas of the LMS in northern England was the worst in living memory. There were some tremendous snow-blocks in the Peak District, but conditions on the Settle and Carlisle line were the worst ever. For more than a fortnight the line was completely blocked by gigantic snowdrifts between the northern end of Blea Moor tunnel and Kirkby Stephen, and one drift near Dent station was estimated to stand between 38 and 40 feet high. All traffic from Leeds to the north was routed from Settle Junction, via the moorland Clapham Junction, Ingleton, Low Gill and thence over Shap. It is a matter of history that even in the worst times of winter storms the LNW line was able to keep going, while the Midland was blocked. In February 1947 the LMS wanted the government in London to know what conditions were like north of Settle, and a photographer well known to railway enthusiasts of thirty years ago, W. Hubert-Foster, was taken up to Dent. He wrote an entertaining and finely illustrated article in the short-lived periodical *Railway Pictorial*, Spring 1947. His photographs were shortly afterwards presented at a meeting of the Cabinet in Downing Street.

55. Developments in Class 5 4–6–0s under Ivatt – engine no. 4748, first of a batch of ten with Caprotti valve gear.

The summer of 1947 was a time when modernists were urging upon railway managements the need to modernise motive power. Attention was repeatedly drawn to the speed with which the American railways were changing over to diesel traction, and on all hands there was the cry that steam was antiquated and should be displaced as soon as possible. On the LMS H. G. Ivatt determined upon a scientific comparison of the economics of steam versus diesel traction in heavy main line service by purchase, from the English Electric Co. Ltd, of two diesel-electric locomotives of a power that would enable direct comparison of running costs and general performance with standard steam locomotives. It was intended that these comparisons should be comprehensive and prolonged, to determine whether a wider introduction of diesel main line power

56. The one Class 5 4–6–0 built with outside Stephenson link motion, no. 4767, built at Crewe in 1947, and now preserved in running order.

was economically justified. The steam loco-motive designs against which the diesels would be compared were the Duchess class 4–6–2, running between Euston and Glasgow, and the 'Black Five' 4–6–0 on the Midland line. Two diesel-electric locomotives, each of 1600 engine horsepower were ordered from the English Electric Company. For the heaviest West Coast express services, in competition with Duchess class 4–6–2s, the two diesel locomotives would be coupled in multiple to provide 3200 horse-power, while on the Midland line they would be used singly.

At the same time, Mr Ivatt appreciated that the 'Black Five' would remain the principal workhorse for many years to come. In the authorisations he had to build many more of them, he decided to include a number of vari-ations from the well-tried Stanier design. Some were fitted with Timken roller bearing axle

57. The first British diesel-electric main line locomotive, LMS no. 10000, just before leaving St Pancras on a test run to Manchester. Mr H. G. Ivatt is climbing down from the cab.

boxes to the coupled wheels; some were subjected to considerable changes in detail design in order to include the Caprotti valve gear, and most interesting of all, one was fitted with the Stephenson's link motion outside. In addition, six of the new locomotives were to be fitted with twin-orifice blastpipes and double chimneys. The thirty new locomotives were divided as follows:

Numbers	Valve Gear	Coupled Wheel Bearings
4738 to 4747	Caprotti	Plain
4748 to 4757	Caprotti	Timken roller
4758 to 4766	Walschaert	Timken roller
4767	Stephenson (outside)	Timken roller

The Stephenson link motion engine, no. 4767, was one of those fitted with the double chimney. Two new 4–6–2 locomotives were also completed in this final year of the LMS – no. 6256, 'Sir William A. Stanier FRS', and no. 6257, 'City of Salford'. They incorporated the new standard arrangement of rocking grate, self-emptying ashpan and self-cleaning smokebox that had been incorporated in three Pacifics built in 1946, but on nos 6256 and 6257 *all* axles of the engine and tender were fitted with roller bearings. The trailing truck of the engines was redesigned as a one-piece steel casting. These two locomotives, incorporating all the latest refinements in steam locomotive design, were intended for direct comparison, on all counts, with the new diesels. Though in 1947 schedules on the West Coast Main Line, as mentioned earlier, were still much decelerated, and did not

58. The two diesel-electrics, nos 10001 and 10000, leaving Euston on a down Anglo-Scottish express shortly after nationalisation.

require anything like a full capacity performance from locomotives of such power as the Duchesses.

With vesting date for nationalisation fixed for 1 January 1948 everyone who was interested in transport eagerly awaited news of appointments, first to the British Transport Commission and then to the Railway Executive. It was no longer a matter for chairmen and boards of directors. They were to disappear overnight. The appointments to the British Transport Commission, only five members, were made by the Minister of Transport, Alfred Barnes. As Michael Bonavia has written in his book *The Birth of British Rail*: 'He had had no previous involvement in transport and merely stuck to the task laid down for him in the party manifesto and in the briefs written for him by his civil servants – treating the whole vast operation as a chore to be performed without complaint.' With a distinguished civil servant, Sir Cyril Hurcomb, as Chairman, the only representative of the main line railways on the Commission, if one excepts a former General

R. G. Jarvis, courtesy Millbrook House Ltd.

59. First of the new Class 4F 2–6–0s, built in 1947 with all modern improvements.

Secretary of the NUR, was Sir William Wood; but although LMS men might have been gratified that their top executive had been so chosen, without the support of his former headquarters organisation – so assiduously built up on the principles laid down by Lord Stamp – he did not prove very effective.

The next tier downwards in the new management structure, the men who had really got to do the job, gave a much more positive indication of how things would develop in the immediate future, and it was clear from the outset that LMS influence would be strong. It was the intention that the posts concerning engineering and operation, together with commercial aspects of traffic, should be divided between the four formerly private railways. Although Riddles was by no means the most senior of the mechanical engineers in 1947, his career, both on the LMS and in government service, had shown his ability as engineer and administrator, and he was appointed Member for mechanical and electrical engineering. On the operating side V. M. Barrington-Ward of the LNER was an obvious choice, from his able conduct of the same job over the whole of the British railways during the war. From the LMS point of view his appointment was not likely to involve any change. In his previous post as Superintendent in the Southern Area of the LNER he had used the Midland system of traffic control, rather than the graphic methods of the North Eastern and Scottish Areas. In the first set-up of the Railway Executive signalling came under the Member for Civil Engineering, J. C. L. Train, of the LNER with the pedestrian H. H. Dyer, formerly an assistant in the LMS signal department, as executive officer.

60. One of the new Class 4F 2–6–0s, numbered M3006, after nationalisation, climbing the Grayrigg bank near Hay Fell box.

F. R. Hebron, Rail Archive Stephenson

Railway enthusiasts were naturally most interested in the prospects for new locomotives, and beneath Riddles the influence was duly revealed to be almost entirely LMS. While to those whose affections lay elsewhere this appeared to be pure and unreasoning bias there is no question that in all the circumstances it was

the correct move. Not all the former railway companies were so co-operative as the LMS in helping to set up the new organisation. In some areas senior officers just did not want to know, and on that score alone bringing to the new headquarters staff men who would be apt to rock the boat would be difficult. But quite apart from questions of personality the organisation of the LMS mechanical and electrical engineering department was unquestionably the most soundly based of the four, resulting from the great leadership of Sir William Stanier and his skill not only in organising first-class production methods but in building up a strong and united team. So, from Derby went R. C. Bond, to become Chief Officer, Locomotive Works; E. Pugson, to be responsible for carriage and wagon construction and maintenance, and E. S. Cox, to be Executive Officer, Design. Only Charles Cock, formerly Chief Electrical Engineer of the Southern, came from outside the LMS enclave. When Barrington-Ward in his operating organisation chose Harold Rudgard to be chief of motive power it did indeed seem as though everything to do with locomotives was to be nearly, if not quite 'closed shop' for the LMS.

Yet the last entirely new locomotive design that came out of Derby, just in time to carry the initials LMS on its tender, was curiously unsuccessful at first. This was the Class 4F 2–6–0, an engine that ran Bulleid's austerity 0–6–0 on the Southern very close for the distinction of the ugliest ever. In some areas the new 4Fs were nicknamed 'Doodle bugs'. With 17½ in. by 26 in. cylinders, 5 ft 3 in. coupled wheels, and 225 lb. per sq. in. pressure they were basically powerful engines, and to provide maximum accessibility the running plate was pitched very high, with all the 'works' gauntly exposed. But despite the modern provision of a twin-orifice blastpipe and double chimney those original engines of 1947 just would not steam. I had some footplate runs with them over the heavily graded Somerset and Dorset line, and it was always a case of the fireman 'fiddling' his way, turning off the injectors periodically, and one usually topped Masbury summit, even with pilot assistance, with boiler pressure down to about 150 lb. per sq. in., instead of 225. After

nationalisation the double chimneys were replaced by single ones and the draughting modified, and they became excellent engines.

The last month of the existence of the LMS was marked by pageantry in the locomotive department. In the first week of that rather sad December of 1947 the first main line diesel-electric locomotive to run on a British railway was driven out of the paint shop at Derby by Ivatt himself, to the cheers of the men who had helped to build her. No. 10000 was finished in black, but her number and the initials LMS were displayed on her flanks in stainless steel characters, riveted to the body sides. As R. C. Bond once remarked: 'We did not intend that the origin of the first main line diesel locomotive built by a British railway company should be easily obliterated, or forgotten.' A few days later she came to Euston for inspection by the board and also to stand alongside one of the two last Pacifics, the nameplate of which was to be ceremonially unveiled by the Chairman. I need hardly add that the Pacific in question was no. 6256, 'Sir William A. Stanier FRS', and that its namesake, Sir William himself, retired, but very hale and hearty, was there to enjoy it all.

And so the quarter-century of LMS history ended. It is a history of great men and great technological advance. One thinks of Granet, Stamp, Reid, Hartley; of Byrom, Malcolm Speir, Pope, Stanier and many others. From a muddled agglomeration in 1923 the LMS grew to be one of the greatest and most forward looking railway entities anywhere in the world, and second to none – if not actually without rivals – in most engineering spheres. It was strangely enough only in signalling that it lagged behind, though in safety in operation its standards were of the highest. That it steamed into the new era with so many of its leading men taking top positions was significant of the stature it had attained.

Index